YOU HAVE
PERMISSION

To Live Your Heart's Desire

Lisa M. Gulland-Nelson

YOU HAVE PERMISSION

Copyright © 2020 Lisa M. Gulland-Nelson

All rights reserved.

No part of this publication may be reproduced, distributed, or transmitted in any form or by any means, including photocopying, recording, or other electronic or mechanical methods, without the prior written permission of the publisher, except in the case of brief quotations embodied in critical reviews and certain other noncommercial uses permitted by copyright law.

Design by Transcendent Publishing

ISBN: 978-1-7353738-7-4

Printed in the United States of America.

Dedication

*T*o my mother, JoAnn; my grandmothers, Erma and Amanda; my Aunt Diane; my great-grandmother, Gertrude Fiedler; and all the women past and present who have won their own battles, inner and outer, who have paved the way with their blood, sweat and tears.

We are one story with many chapters.

Below is an excerpt from the Life of Gertrude Fieldler, written by Diane (Gulland) Knutson, my aunt who passed away after a brave battle with cancer just as I was finishing the edits to this book. ...

> *Gertrude Fiedler, daughter of Martin & Margaret Fiedler, was born in Dent, Minnesota. She was the youngest of eight children and the only girl. Her father was a country doctor and farmer.*
>
> *She married Emil R. Krueger on December 5th, 1897. They farmed near Amenia, North Dakota until 1942 when they retired and moved to Casselton.*
>
> *Emil & Gertrude had ten children: Roy, Walter, Hulda, Adolph, Helen, Amanda, William, Clarence (my grandfather), Robert and Arthur.*
>
> ...

Gertrude was blessed with many talents. Besides raising a large family, she was a master of needlework. Gertrude could watch tv or look out the window and her hands were busy crocheting. She made up many of her own stitches. She crocheted boxes of baby sweaters, caps and booties for the Children's Home in Fargo.

She had an amazing green thumb and loved to raise African Violets. She made African Violet baskets, a complete ball of violets.

When Grandma left the farm, she gave away one of her favorite plants, an oleander. After coming to live with us, she was given a start off that original plant. It sat next to the window beside her. She watered it, pruned it and loved it. She even talked to it, but alas it would not bloom. She just could not figure out why it would not bloom. The day of her funeral, when we walked into the living room, there by the window next to her chair was one single white oleander bloom. I believe she was blooming in heaven and was letting us know.

She was always amazed that she had lived from covered wagons to airplanes and traveled in both.

She will always be in our hearts.

To all the women in our hearts, the ones who've paved the way, the ones who've lived their dreams and the ones who've boxed up their dreams to do for others. For the women who've passed on and whose souls send us love, push us quietly and whisper in our ears, "Go now, child, and be the light you were meant to be." This book is dedicated to them. They are the love that lifts us up when we are ready to call it quits, and they are the gentle light that touches our hearts when we are soaring high. They are love. And we are blessed.

Table of Contents

Chapter 1. You Deserve to be Happy. 1

Chapter 2. The Gift of the Present Moment 11

Chapter 3. The Science of Energy – It's All There Is. 23

Chapter 4. Watch Your Vibe 33

Chapter 5. Time for Women to Rise 41

Chapter 6. Being an Example. 51

Chapter 7. Other's Light, Your heart 55

Chapter 8. Go Easy, Love 65

Chapter 9. The Art of Saying No. 75

Chapter 10. Your Rules 79

Chapter 11. Your Life Brought You Here. 87

Chapter 12. Life Reflects What You Need 95

Chapter 13. Owning Your Truth 103

Chapter 14. Create Your Own Circle of Wisdom 109

Introduction

"In every community, there is work to be done. In every nation, there are wounds to heal. In every heart there is the power to do it."

~**Marianne Williamson.**

Why am I writing this book? And what do I know?

*I*t started long ago, with little questions, comments that sparked epiphanies, an internal knowing here and there. But I think my journey into "the meaning of life" really started when my parents died. When that happened, I was left with fear and questions I couldn't answer. More than anything I wanted to feel a little more secure, and for me that meant finding ways to better understand something. I wanted to know things like: *What happens when we die?* and *"What's "out there?"* That quickly led to, *Why are we here?* and *What is the purpose?*, which in turn led to still more questions. This was my admission to "spiritual college," and I've been there ever since – asking questions and finding answers, which then revealed more questions and oftentimes some fear as well. Whenever I uncovered a fear or doubt, well, that's when I knew I was really getting to something, uncovering the real dirt, if you will.

Slowly, I started tiptoeing through these fears and doubts, just as one walks through a minefield. Through the fears of dying, fears of spirits, and past life issues that were affecting me in ways I couldn't even come close to understanding. I grew up Lutheran, so past lives weren't exactly part of my belief system. Sometimes the concept is still hard to totally grasp or believe yet releasing past-life blocks has undeniably been a huge part of my healing. Is it a placebo effect? It could be, but I don't think so; either way, it has been working so, who cares? If past lives resonate with you, great. If not, that's okay too. We each have our own path to healing.

I also didn't set out to write this book; it snuck up on me when I was least expecting. My plan was to write a sweet novel about a young girl and her adventure. Instead, you're getting *my* adventure. I've been plagued with doubts throughout this process: *Who am I, and what do I know? Who wants to listen to me? Who even likes me?* But then, that's the point. Aren't those the doubts we all have in some way, shape or form? And that's the heart of it. That's the dirt, the soil we can work with for our nourishment and growth. But I'm getting ahead of myself.

This book, at its core, is about finding and maintaining balance, both as individual and as part of the collective. This is especially needed for women, for we give so much of ourselves (often too much) because we have internalized the belief that it is through our sacrifice that we do good in the world. I, however, am starting to believe it's quite the opposite. What we are really doing with all this sacrifice is creating an imbalance. Everything is energy and energy requires balance. For us humans, that energy is represented in the masculine and the feminine. The masculine side manifests as the tendency to create and protect; the feminine side is intuition (or "knowing") and allowing. Somewhere along the line we have forgotten how to create and maintain that balance, and this is what we must remember if we ever hope to heal ourselves and the world.

That is my mission, to help others awaken the feminine energies within themselves so that we can all step into our power and live a

Introduction

heart-centered life. When we do, we will find that our true work is to not sacrifice ourselves, but to show ourselves the kindness usually reserved for others. It is from this place of wholeness that kindness toward others will naturally flow. In other words, by finding balancing and healing ourselves we will help balance and heal a world that sorely needs both.

So what do you do to find this balance, this healing? The answer may surprise you: you do nothing. That's right; you don't do, you *be*. You are already a healer, a nurturer, a birther of ideas. Your smile, your laughter and your kind energy light up the world. And that is enough. You are already enough, just by virtue of your existence here on Earth. *Take a moment and let that settle down into your bones and down to your soul.* And when we can heal our hurts, bring forth our visions and find what truly gives us peace and joy, we will see our world shift into balance. And while the shift may be a little (or a lot) uncomfortable, on the other side awaits peace, love and, that seemingly elusive happiness. Now, I challenge you to make your light a little brighter still by doing more to nurture yourself and your ideas so you can give even more light and love to the world. I believe the one thing, the only thing, that will save this world, is a whole and peace-filled you. Nothing less, simply…you.

If this is difficult to wrap your arms around, imagine tossing a pebble into a pond. The ripple appears small, but it creates waves that affect the whole pond. The waves hit the shore, shifting the soil, and the seeds take root. Those seeds germinate, growing into trees that create and support abundant life. One small shift creates one change that leads to another. They are changes you may never see. Like the pebble, our seemingly small actions can create little changes that turn into big change as they ripple into other parts of our lives, then out into the world. Even while your head is turned or while you're relaxing on your couch with a good book, your actions, large and small, have begun a chain reaction. Let's say that you have been inspired to change your life, to just do one small thing differently, something for yourself. You tell a friend about it, and she's inspired to do something different and brave, something that makes her happier. She talks to her aunt, who lives in another country, and the aunt is now inspired to do something brave or change her life. Each woman's actions ripple out to improve the lives of those around her and on it goes. These seemingly insignificant things pile up and begin to change an entire country. The changes take a country from one of oppression to one of independence. Now, it may feel like a long way to go from a chat with a friend to changing a country, but when you consider that everything we do is like tossing one little pebble out, you will start to see how these changes begin to alter the landscape of our lives.

Here is an example from my own life. When I saw a gap in my daughter's school, I started asking questions and was connected to certain resources. I asked some more questions and was able to help start a pilot program called Mentors in Math. College students, including engineering and other majors, would spend a little time each week mentoring second graders in math. It was a great program, and I was just excited to have the opportunity to get the right people together, have teachers willing to try something new and get this in front of the kids. The Mentors in Math program inspired another woman to create a summer camp for kids who have long-term illnesses or spend a lot of time in hospitals. The camp was intended to provide them with a support system and connect them with other kids who may have similar experiences. I couldn't believe the project I did inspired someone else to create something needed out there, but it did. And I believe the ripples keep going. We don't need to force anything, just let our ideas take us along the river of our life.

The question is, what kind of change do we want to make? What kind of world do we want reflecting back to us? These are the questions I hope this book will help you answer, or at least start thinking about in a new way.

So, let's travel on together, my friend. We've got some work to do. I'm blessed to join you on a small part of your journey. We are soul sisters and, this book, this outpouring of my heart and soul, is my gift to you. I hope my journey can help unlock parts of yours. When we can walk together, the journey becomes a little less difficult and a little sweeter. May your journey be blessed. Allow abundance and allow your soul to breathe, sing and dance in its ever-unfoldingness. This life is about growth, but it can be growth in joy and ease. Remember that. Write in on your hand. *This life is meant to be easy and filled with joy, and you deserve it. Yes, you have permission to be happy.*

Chapter 1

You Deserve to be Happy

Now we get into the nitty gritty of it. What are we doing on this planet? What do we deserve, and are we truly living up to our own divine potential? And, perhaps more important than all of that, are we truly happy? Why does that matter? Well, as I mentioned earlier, it's because I believe our happiness will "ripple out" to create a world that reflects such happiness back to us. Many spiritual leaders and ascended masters have focused on inner peace as a path to creating peace and happiness in our outer world. Essentially, world peace begins by finding inner peace. As within so without. This brings us to the question, Do you know how to be happy? And by this I mean *happy*, not simply complacent or even content. Do you know how to follow your heart's desire? Do you even know what is contained within your heart? At first, this may seem like an odd question, but the truth is that many of us spend so much time pretending that others' happiness is our own that we've lost the ability to hear the voice of our heart. We've given our ego/mind the reins for so long that we no longer hear our heart's voice. In other words, we are out of balance. Yes, we need our ego because we live in a world full of "contrast," a concept discussed by Abraham Hicks (among others).

Contrast are those things we would classify as unwanted in our lives, however according to Abraham, they come to us as a lesson. We tend to see only the good as worthy of our appreciation. Sometimes, it's the really "awful" things that give us the greatest growth. And if nothing else, they allow us to see what we don't want. We can't always be sure where we are going if all roads look the same. We need a wrong path to show us the right path, don't we? When you look at the "bad" that has happened, you can be grateful for what it's taught you. Contrast shows you what happens when you put your focus toward what you don't want. It is by focusing on what we do want, by listening to the wisdom of our heart, our soul, our higher self, that we will arrive on the path to happiness.

It's time to wake up, to give ourselves permission to create as much happiness as our beautiful hearts can stand and then create a little more. Let's allow ourselves to believe in the power of our happiness to cause the ripple effect, extending well beyond ourselves. Allow yourself to feel the energy of hope, love and abundance. Remember that you have a right to all of that and more. It is your birthright. It is your truth, if you accept it. And only if you accept it.

The world sorely needs more love, inspired ideas and kindness, and it starts with the kindness we owe ourselves. For far too long we have given too much to make others' dreams come true. We are finally starting to realize that we do not need to sacrifice our dreams, but rather in achieving them we can create so much space and light that it makes the dreams of others manifest that much faster. So, let's take a little more time to be kind to ourselves and watch as the world reflects our creation and energy. Truly, it will.

The Dalai Lama said, "The world will be saved by the Western Woman." I believe that's true, and I also believe that the world will be saved because we finally decided to heal ourselves. It's our inner healing that will heal the world — it is how we will create heaven on Earth. As above, so below.

How do we heal? We heal by going right to the source of our pain. We heal by letting our heart guide us to our feelings, then by finally listening to them. We embrace and welcome the thunderstorm of healing tears, and we dance to the lava hot rage that flows forth. We give it space and allow it to speak to us, then release it, layer by layer, shaking ourselves free from the past. It takes courage, and I know you've got an abundance of that.

Dive into the pain your heart holds and feel it so you can release it...

One night, I was giving myself time to process the pain that I'd pushed down into the dark depths of my heart, so far down that I thought it didn't exist. Both of my parents died of cancer, but my father's quick but painful transition had particularly affected me. When our local hospital had done all they could, they sent him to The Mayo Clinic in Minneapolis, which was about three hours away from my home. One day I left his room just for a minute, and that was when the doctor came in and told him there was nothing more they could do.

I sat with my dad as he fought to eat soup, his hand shaking as he slowly moved the spoon from the bowl to his mouth. He was too damn stubborn to let me help him, though he did confess that he was scared and not ready to die. That conversation would stay with me, rolling around my head over and over, long after he had passed. Each time I imagined myself giving him some profound healing message when in actuality I'd said nothing. There were so many things in my heart, but the words just didn't make it out of my mouth. Later, the pain of things left unsaid would continue to weigh heavily on me, though I didn't always realize this was where it came from. It was as if the pain was locked behind the door to my heart. Now I was finally ready to open that door and let the light in.

I imagined the door opened to a small cabin that was quaint and charming but full of dust and neglect. I can start here, I tell myself.

I can dig in and get dirty and cough from the dust of pain and loss, knowing that my tears heal. I can remember we are eternal, and that there is no death, not really, just the illusion of death we experience while in this matrix. I can remember that my dad and my loved ones are right here in my heart so I can let go and allow them to speak to me. For me, that healing sometimes starts best with memories. And when I step into that dusty little room of emotion and let it all rise up, I realize that the pain came from the resistance. It's not painful to cry. It feels good. It is painful before I cry, before I let go and fall into it. And sometimes, we fear that once we fall, we'll never be able to climb our way out of the pain. The allowing is always scarier than the doing; trusting the process is what takes courage. The only way out is through. We won't get lost in the abyss; we'll find the diamond of our true self.

So how do we get down to those subconscious hurts, fears and beliefs? Sometimes, they are buried so deeply we have no idea they are there until they manifest in our bodies as physical illness. Certainly our ego does everything it can to keep us from them, for it believes that when we heal and shed those beliefs, fears and junk holding us back, we will shed it as well. This is why we must go in with the strength of compassion and be gentle with our ego, parenting it, even as we start to call in our higher self, our soul, to help us heal. Our soul will remind us who we truly are, revealing the deepest most beautiful, profound truth of ourselves. We are not here to play small or to hide. We are here to shine in our magnificence.

We have a right to answer the call of our heart and say, *I must do this because it is needed for my soul – be it a college degree, a coffee date or just a nap.* We have a right and an obligation to say yes to our heart, to demand what brings us to life.

This should be common sense, so why does it feel "off" for so many of us? Why does it feel uncomfortable or even scary when it comes to saying no to something so we can say yes to ourselves? The answer is programming. Think about how long women have been told to put others ahead of themselves (literally, it's been millennia!). Think about how we have internalized this programming. And it's okay; no one knew better. There is no judgement. However, now we must give ourselves permission to get to the core of the faulty beliefs that are keeping us from really stepping into our true heart's desire.

Secret Garden

Let's imagine that deep inside ourselves there is a secret garden. We all have our own unique garden, known only to us, and it is perfect and radiant, exactly what we would expect. This secret garden is hidden deep inside our soul, and it reflects all the hopes, dreams and aspirations we hold dear. It holds our soul's mission and the love we brought here from the creative source, from God. Your garden contains all the dreams you had as a child and all the dreams you've had since. It holds the true mission you came here to fulfill. Think back to when you were a child, and you sat in your favorite spot and daydreamed without limit. What did you dream about? Where did you see yourself going? What did you see yourself becoming? All of those hopes and dreams were the seeds to a secret garden hidden deep within your soul. Your garden holds the potential for boundless beauty and a life unlimited.

Do you know what your garden contains? What condition it's in? Perhaps it is so hidden that you don't even know where to begin looking. Everything you've ever wanted for yourself is in that garden. And if you don't remember what you want, or if you don't know where your garden is or what it might contain, that's okay. Simply begin from where you are right now and set your intention to begin to remember. Soon you will come to find your garden, one step at a time, one thought at a time. You'll find the place inside you that has safely nurtured or hidden your dreams, protecting it from all your fears and negative belief patterns. It's the place that reflects the beauty of your love and the manifestation of your greatest, most treasured desire.

It's no wonder that so many of our gardens are hidden. In the best of times, women have been taught that their dreams must take a back seat. At the very worst, we've been persecuted for our strengths, hung, tortured and burned at the stake. Either way, this repression of our needs has taken a toll on our psyche.

Our gardens didn't start out all grown-over and full of weeds. They started with beautiful buds, fresh little greens and flowers delicately growing up from the beautiful depths of our souls. As children, we were able to nurture and love each and every fresh little bud, believing in ourselves and our dreams. Then, little by little, well-intentioned adults and loved ones started to create doubt that put shadows on every little flower until they could no longer flourish. It was the aunt who said, "No, honey, girls don't do that, go help your mamma"; the friend who gave you a look when you wore that one outfit; the adult who told you not to cry because you were embarrassing them; and so on. For the most part, the people in our lives said those things because they were trying to protect us, to steer us along the right path, to teach us how to survive in this world. "Go to school but study the right things"; "Wear this but not that"; "Say this but never that"; "Make sure you are enough but not too much." Whatever the intention, these words of advice boxed us in, held us back and taught us to be less than who we are. What's more, we've bought into the oppression so much that we've started to believe it's not only correct, but what we want. We've started to believe that over-giving is our strength. I say this not to judge, but to point out that it's time for a change. Slowly but surely, we *are* changing it. Brave women have fought and clawed their way to equality. Women have said, "I deserve this; I am paving the way for all women to say, 'Yes, me too.'"

Now is the time to step into our own power and step out of our comfort zones in order to change the status quo. The biggest challenge we face is changing our own beliefs. It's about the willingness to take that first step, whatever that first step is. It will take time and slow deliberate tending to uncover the beautiful garden that hides deep within our souls. It could be no other way. It's not something that we can uncover overnight because we didn't bury it overnight. In fact, the "burying" happened over lifetimes. Lifetimes of traditions, beliefs and actions handed down and weaved into truth. Thankfully, it won't take lifetimes to heal. With a little time and love, we will bask in the beauty of our dreams in full bloom.

Maybe it is time to try the path less traveled. Maybe it's time to grab a hatchet and chop your way through the thick dense forest to forge your own unique path. And just maybe on the other side of the dark, thick underbrush, you'll find a beauty that is too splendid and too beautiful to be believed. Maybe you'll find the most beautiful, strongest, most fully realized version of you waiting there.

Past Lives and Our Healing

How many lives do we live, and if we live more than this current life what does that mean for our healing journey?

Indeed, there is evidence to suggest we live hundreds if not thousands of lives as part of our soul's growth and evolution. There are numerous books and articles on the topic, including accounts of young children who recall very specific details about past incarnations, details like house numbers, their names, what they looked like, and how they died. Investigations into these claims, often resulting in findings that they are valid.

Renowned hypnotherapist and author Michael Newton has presented groundbreaking discoveries on what happens after we die. His book *Journey of Souls* includes interviews of twenty-nine people who, under hypnosis, recall not only their past lives but their experience *in between* lives. Newton also reveals how he initially resisted past life work because it seemed "unorthodoxed and non-clinical." He soon realized, however, that "our deep-seated memories offer a set of past experiences which are too real and connected to be ignored."

While you may or may not (yet) include past lives in your set of beliefs, uncovering and healing past lives has contributed much to my own healing journey. It is certainly not necessary to believe in past lives if it makes you uncomfortable. You can heal all your blocks by working with the experiences in your current life. But for many of us, tapping into experiences from previous lifetimes has been a great way to uncover blocks, thereby revealing more of our true selves.

A few years ago, my husband and I attended a retreat in Sedona. During the event, we did two or three past life sessions. One particular traumatic past life event was emerging throughout the course of the weekend. In fact, my spirit guides or higher self saved the final pieces of the puzzle, revealing them to me on our eighty-minute drive to the airport. This particular past life took place in Egypt, and I was in love with my (current) husband, but he was either of a higher status or was promised to another woman. He loved me too but wouldn't go against the rules. So one night, I rode my black horse to their home, snuck into their room and stabbed both of them with my sword. I watched as he died and drank poison to end my own life.

Now you might say, well, that sounds pretty made up. Normally, I would agree with you but bear with me. First, due to a previous surgery, my husband had been battling a pain on one side of his stomach. The odds of this type of injury were very low. The other woman, who was also attending the retreat, had been battling a similar stomach pain/injury that wouldn't go away. The only difference seemed to be that it was on the opposite side – it was a mirroring pain almost like someone stabbed them with a sword. Finally, when we got home, I felt so much intense emotion that I called the retreat facilitators. They guided me to journal; it helped a little but just wasn't enough. I could barely contain my emotion. Finally, that night when my husband got home, all the pain and emotion flooded out of me, and I cried until there was nothing left.

Since then, I've uncovered and healed many past lives, peeling back and releasing layers of pain and hurt to reveal who I truly am beneath all that density.

It's important to note, that while it can be tempting to want to stay in the world of past lives avoiding the pain or boredom of our current lives, they are only useful for healing blocks. You came here to live this life fully. This is the life that truly matters.

What's holding you back?

At some point in life, the vast majority of us have been held back by something. Maybe it's a fear of seeing something we don't want to see or dealing with something we've safely tucked away. Or maybe, it is a fear of *being seen*, because once people really see us, they can see our perceived flaws as well. Every crack in our armor, every jagged rough patch, all the ways we've failed (or, maybe worse, they'll see our perfection). We all have skeletons in our closets and yucky, black tar-filled doubts about so many things. We have questions about things we "shouldn't" question, like religion or some other taboo topic. But when we take a topic off the table, when we take away our right to question even basic things, we take ourselves out of the game. Our intuition is guiding us to those questions; they are how we move ourselves into our heart, how we grow. And it's how we level the playing field and bring this beautiful Mother Earth back into balance.

Sure, those questions may cause some fear inside of us, as all change does. But don't mistake the fear of an exciting new discovery and expansion for the fear your body would use to alert you that there's a tiger about to eat you. The former is just your ego and ages and ages of suppression confusing you about what it means to be safe. The latter is warning you to get the hell out of there before you get devoured.

Another big fear we have is letting go. We might have an unconscious belief that we are unworthy or unsafe. But those times are over and really were never true. Our light, our energy, our soul is eternal. We are safe to be who we are. We are safe to ask questions. We are safe to get angry, to swear, to cry and to walk the fuck away. We are safe to take time for ourselves to fill our own cup right back up to its tippy top! We are safe to honor our own path, whatever that path is.

If we ask those questions, the Universe will answer us; we must simply be willing to listen, and to understand that those answers may come in unexpected ways. In fact, I'm willing to bet that if you look back at your life, you'll find that the Universe always answered your questions in many different and unique ways. It may have come, for example, in the form of a book a friend randomly recommended, or a song on the radio. The next step is to trust the answers the Universe is giving us, rather than allowing fear to block the truth. One way we can move through those fear blocks is to ask our spirit guides or angels to make the answers so clear or so repetitive that we can neither deny them nor mistake them for a "coincidence." It takes courage and patience to call the truth into you, to trust it and face it. There is no wrong way, so be kind and patient with yourself and the process. You will cry; you will heal old wounds. You will see that the real source of your pain was your own resistance. You will come to realize that your healing is balm for the world.

Chapter 2

The Gift of the Present Moment

*A*s we begin to cultivate our garden, working to uncover the dreams we had as a child or those we've been afraid to shine our light on, it's helpful to be present in the moment. When we focus on what is right before us, we aren't as prone to worrying about the future or regretting the past. We are in our power. If we can simply be in the now, doing what makes us happy, our happiness will act as a conduit, bringing forth the things we really want to create. We can get more of what we want by doing more of what makes us happy. It's really that simple! When we do that, we allow a path to unfold that takes us closer to whatever it is we need to cultivate or to uncover what's in that garden.

We have countless reminders every day to live in the present moment, many of them concerning things we consider mundane. For example, have you ever tried to boil milk to make oatmeal? It's a tricky business. You have to stick with it, be present. I have a difficult time boiling milk without having it spill all over. I'm there at the beginning, patiently stirring, waiting for the milk to start boiling. I have my oatmeal all measured out and ready. Then I get a little distracted, something happens, or I just want to, really quickly, take care of something else. Sometimes it is quick, sometimes it's not. Either way, it almost never fails, the moment I step away is the moment the milk starts to boil. And once it starts, man, it goes fast. Before you know it, the milk has boiled over the edge of the pot. It makes a huge mess, and milk stinks when it burns.

Life can be one big pot of milk at times. We tend to it. We believe we are being patient. Then, right when the fun is about to happen, we walk away, give up or move on. Do you allow yourself to be patient, trust the process and wait for the blessings to really bubble up? If we give ourselves permission to be patient with the process, we allow the results to come when they may. I truly believe that when we focus on the joy of it all, the results come to us much faster than we could imagine. As we get older, it can be as much about overthinking as lack of patience. We hold a belief that life should be difficult, complicated or stressful, and because we believe it, we make it so. We miss the wonder of the present moment.

Take this scenario. You are on vacation, and it's a beautiful morning. You're at the beach and the sun is up, not a single cloud in the sky and it's going to be a perfect day. You distractedly notice the sun and the beauty of the morning, but it doesn't sink in. You glance at it, yes, but give it no notice. You are thinking about what time the kids will wake up and where you will have breakfast. You're thinking about which swimsuits they will want to wear and can't forget the sunscreen and towels! Is the bag big enough? Should we sign up for that excursion? Will little Susie make it, or should just hubby and the older kids go? Where did Johnny put his towel from yesterday? It has to get hung up or it won't dry, and on and on.

Is it just me, or did you go from the calm beauty to feeling stressed in those few short sentences? The difference is palpable, even in the made-up scenario. The beautiful morning is gone, replaced by chaos in the form of your family arriving (or merely your thoughts about their anticipated arrival). Of course, all your worrying doesn't change

The Gift of the Present Moment

a thing about how the day unfolds. You don't eat breakfast where you thought. Your kids all go and your husband winds up taking the middle child, not the youngest, back to the hotel room. You worried through an opportunity to appreciate the moment. On the other hand, you have gained another opportunity to learn.

What do I mean by this?

While it is important to live in the present, the past can be a helpful tool to see how far we have come. When we look back in a healthy, non-judgmental way (for example, how we wasted a beautiful morning on vacation), we can recognize the beauty of the journey itself. We can see the beauty in the chaos. Think about every big or even some of the smaller accomplishments in your life. It has always been the journey that's been the most important, the most memorable. You can see how each step, even the painful ones, unfolded in the most perfect way.

The question is, can we take each moment one by one and let the love of chaos enfold us? Can we allow life to simply unfold? Can we trust the Universe to bring us everything that is of our highest good? What might happen if we stopped worrying about all those things? I don't mean stop doing, just stop worrying. What might happen if we start allowing the best outcome and when something shows up to provide contrast (meaning an example of what we don't want), simply appreciate it and move on to what we love, what's working. Besides, isn't "contrast" what gives us the best stories, like the time you were visiting that big city and got on the wrong bus, circling around everywhere with your in-laws? (Yep, that happened, and the Canadian bus driver didn't care one bit for the frazzled Americans.) Those are the stories that make you laugh…later. If we can begin to add in a little trust that it will all work out — maybe not as we expect but as it should for our highest good — we might find ourselves gliding along this life more beautifully than we could ever imagine. Start out by giving it just one day. If that works, give it a second day and so on.

One day, I was walking down the street, singing *Doo ah ditty* (just kidding!) and I saw a woman was walking the opposite way. She was looking at her phone as she walked and she did not look up, not even once as she walked the length of the sidewalk. It's easy to understand the temptation. I've done it myself (though not that effectively; I would trip if I didn't look up once in a while). Most of us are so tied up with technology — on social media, answering texts or emails — that we miss a tremendous amount of beauty in the world and in our lives. The day of my walk, the sun was shining, flowers were blooming and birds were chirping, and that woman missed it all. This is how many of us show up for life these days — heads down, moving along, never once looking up. We tend to do what we've always done, without question, and then wonder why nothing changes. Creating what we want may seem impossible, but the truth is one adjustment could be all it takes to change the trajectory of our life; it can be the pebble that creates ripples all around us. We can kick up precious little seeds that grow into a beautiful garden of our life.

Setting Our Intentions

Ask yourself, do you live on purpose, or do you allow life to take you along, with no participation on your part? It's all about intention. For example, my mornings can be complete chaos, or a calming foundation for my day. I have two kids, so sometimes the "chaos mornings" are just a part of life, like when everyone is tired and moving slowly, then suddenly it's a mad dash to get out the door. This used to be frustrating, until I learned that I cannot always control how my morning (or life) will go, but I can control how I react. I took a wonderful class, where the teacher provided tools to help us be more intentional about our day. These tools don't have to take a long time, but they work best when we include our mind, body and soul.

What does that look like? For the body, it's a little movement, maybe a quick walk or some yoga. Maybe it's five minutes or a full-on, get sweaty exercise routine, whatever makes you feel the best. For the soul, it means including some inspiration like listening to something uplifting or reading an uplifting book. For the mind, it means setting your intentions for the day. You could write down things you are grateful for or how you expect your day to go. We're talking positive stuff here, obviously! The whole process doesn't need to take more than twenty minutes. A ten-minute walk while listening to something uplifting and a one-page journal entry about gratitude or positive affirmations is a great way to start your day. Then, if (or, more accurately, when) chaos happens, you can take three deeps breaths and give yourself a minute to appreciate the gift within the craziness.

We can be intentional about how we view whatever the world gives us, understanding that *we* put it there for our own soul's growth. And, yes, we can always find things to be happy about; we can even send love to the things that aren't going well. For one, these things are teaching us something about what we don't want. They are also providing us an opportunity to see our strength. When we can learn to see the gift in these "wrong" things, rather than being bogged down by them, it becomes that much easier to shift our focus to the things that are working. As we cultivate feelings of appreciation and joy, we will find our way to that beautiful garden that much quicker. Once there, we may have to do some weeding, because the garden has been overgrown for a while, but there is no rush. There is no list to complete and no deadline. We allow ourselves time to remove the overgrowth and to let the sunshine in, bringing back to life the dreams we planted there so long ago.

As your garden begins to bloom, you may find yourself spending more and more time there. Before you know it, people begin saying things like, "Wow, what happened to you?" When you ask what they mean, they tell you that you are glowing; they ask if you changed your hair or are using a new skincare product. Or, they may not say anything or even notice the change, but they respond to you differently. Either way, you'll realize that your beauty is coming straight from your secret garden, inside your heart where you've spent time tending, loving and nurturing that which you hold dear. And you will smile and say, "I'm not sure, but enough about me. How are you?"

Let's get focused.

Don't focus on what's *not* good. Don't focus on what's **not** good. Don't focus on what's NOT good. See what I did there? Did you notice where you mind went when I told you not to focus on something? You focused on it! It's important to focus on what we want versus what we don't want. That's because we attract what we are focused on, the same as if we're ordering off a menu. So if we say we don't want to fall, we're still focused on falling. They key is to focus on *keeping our balance.*

If everyone took some time to document the things they focus on during the day, breaking them into "positives" and "negatives," I'm guessing the latter list would be the longer one. How often do we think about what's working or what is fun? How often do we focus on what makes us happy or even what is good about someone else? How often do we think about what makes us come alive – with no limits? And how often do we allow ourselves to JUST get happy? We tend to forget that we have a choice, all the time in every moment, to choose what we think and what we focus on. We tend to believe the thoughts we think are out of our control and dependent upon external circumstances when nothing could be further from the truth.

Half the battle is paying close attention to what we think, and how our thoughts may affect us. Do you know or remember what thoughts have gone through your head in the last hour, or even the last few minutes? If not, you're engaging in lazy thinking. No, this does not mean you're lazy, but like most of us you were never trained to manage your thoughts.

We can focus our thoughts like the captain of our own personal ship, steering ourselves closer to what we want. Conversely, we may think a negative thought and then beat ourselves up for it, which takes us further from what we want. The good news is, it is just a thought; we don't have to own it, and we can simply observe and let it go if it doesn't reflect who we are becoming. We can claim our birthright to be almighty captains, navigating this grand sea of life. We can become intentional about every single thought that goes through our head. It may not happen overnight, and we can practice as long as we need to, a lifetime. That's okay. When we notice a negative thought, we can recognize it and notice the feeling that comes with it. Feel it, and then just release it. Turn our wheel to a new direction and steer into positive thoughts. As we add more positive thoughts and strengthen our ability to become an active participant in our own thinking, the positive thoughts and feelings will automatically take us to where we want to be.

This does not happen overnight. Understanding our thoughts takes great awareness, developed over time, but once we do, we can start to recognize each thought for its whole truth. Like anything else it becomes easier with practice, so be patient with yourself.

The Universe will prove itself if we allow it, and we allow it through the thoughts we think and the words we speak. If we release expectations and limitations on our dreams, the Universe has more abundance, in all forms, than we can often imagine. We are truly the only ones standing in the way of our dreams. We have the life we believe we deserve. So, if we don't like our life, it's time to start believing in our deservingness and telling ourselves a different story. Once we do that, the Universe will deliver it on a silver platter, metaphorically speaking of course.

And the Child Shall Teach Us

So how does one get into the groove of all this? How do we move from not believing, from dwelling in the past or future, to living in the moment and embracing our right to have complete abundance and a heart-driven life? One surefire way is to tap into our inner child.

When I was little, I used to stand on the gravel road on our farm, turn my face up to the sun, and feel God. I knew. I could remember what "home" was like. In time, this knowing started to fade, yet every once in a while, when I turned my face to the sun and just allowed, I would feel that love, peace and pureness. That is what children have that we don't or, more accurately, have forgotten.

Children, whether they are here on earth or our own inner child residing within our heart, remind us of the truth of who we are. We are love in human form, experiencing life on this physical plane. At some point most of us forget this truth, a result of dealing with the trials and density of human existence, however, when we trace our way back to the garden, clean it up and allow it to nourish us, we will remember.

The challenge, for many of us, is to engage our inner child, who has likely been ignored for so long she's either frightened or totally ticked off. Once again, be patient, for it might take some time to get acquainted again. Start by inviting her forward, then listen to her and give her an opportunity to lead you. Set aside a couple of hours a week just for you, then spend this time playing and doing whatever your inner child is urging you to do. Your inner child might urge you to be creative and write or draw. She may urge you to go out in nature and daydream or skip. She might be angry as hell, and you might spend two hours crying, uncovering old hurts ready to be healed. And that's okay! In fact, crying is better than okay. It's a necessary and welcome way to heal. Think of your tears as the rain, bringing your garden back to life. Indulge whatever your inner child wants. Don't overthink it. Just do what feels good to you and allow her to slowly come forward.

When we were young, we went outside. We played and spent time with our favorite people. We journaled, dreamed, laughed. We created,

The Gift of the Present Moment

and we were okay creating not-so-perfect things. We enjoyed learning...about everything. We learned all the time. Then, at some point, many of us sort of stopped all that, and that's when the magic started to fade. We believed that getting older meant becoming serious and stressed and overworked. But is that really what adulthood is supposed to be like? Why can't joy be our goal? If more joy in life could become our primary target, what would change in our own lives and the lives of those around us?

Take some time to consider all the things that bring you joy and all the things that take away your joy. What does that list look like? What things bring you pure joy, and at no "cost" to you? For example, hanging out at a lake on a beautiful sunny day might bring you pure joy, with no price tag, and you don't feel bad later. On the other hand, a night of drinking heavily might give you a certain kind of joy, but you'll most likely pay in the morning, not only the money you spent on cocktails, but the beautiful morning you spend hungover or sleeping. With every action there is a reaction and the more things we do that cause a positive-positive reaction, the happier we will be long term.

Another way to connect with your joy is to learn from the experts: children. Have you spent any time watching a child? If not, and you don't have children of your own, try borrowing one (i.e. a niece, nephew, or the child of a friend). Spend the day doing things the child wants and observe them. If you can, go to the park or be outside. Let the child be your teacher. Go and play. Watch the child as they play and enjoy the present moment. Watch and learn as they release anger, frustration or other emotions through their yells or their tears. They let it out and then they move on, almost as quickly as they started. They don't reflect on it later or talk to their friends about it. They don't complain about it nor do they pretend they're not upset. They just move through it and let it go. They simply experience life. Their joy is pure, their laughter is full, and their hope is unwavering, and yours can be too.

Ask yourself, can you be more childlike? Do you have resistance to that? What thoughts immediately pop up? We may think we are too busy or that we have to take life more seriously than that, but is that really true? Can we do all the things we need to get done without being so serious or without the worry? Can we allow the world to just be, as it is, without complaining, without fighting it or stressing about it? Can we focus more (or solely) on what we love about the world and the people in it, including ourselves? Has any other method really worked anyway?

One day, my son wanted me to play in the sand with him. I said yes because I wanted to spend time with him, but even as I did so my long to-do list was running in the back of my mind. As we played together, my son gave me jobs to do. First, I was to take a shovel and fill in the hole off to the side. I did so quickly and efficiently, then announced, "I'm done." Next, he told me to take the back side of my shovel and flatten and smooth a particular area of sand. I took my shovel and quickly smoothed the area, but this time, when I told him I was done, he replied, "No, you just keep smoothing it." Something about the way he said it made me realize that I was doing it all wrong. It was then that I realized that he was doing these "jobs" for the pure joy of it, not just to get one done so he could move on to the next. He didn't need it to be "done"; he didn't need to accomplish anything; he just was having fun.

Oftentimes we get so caught up in the goal, in finishing something, that we forget to do it just for the joy of doing it. The same is true of life. It's so easy to move from one task to the next, accomplishing and never really enjoying the journey. Next time you wash a dish, try just washing it for the joy of it. Do it slowly and appreciate the dish, the abundance of food that was on it, whatever. Let the joy of doing it be your only "goal."

What if we could commit to a small change? Each day, for about five minutes (more if you can), live like a child. Again, we might need to enlist the help of an expert. No one ever asks them, but children are wise old souls with much to teach and much love to share. Just as my son taught me, one of their most important lessons goes back to simply being happy. Happiness is truly underrated. It's more than just feeling good; it's the ticket to everything we want. It may seem counterintuitive, but happiness will solve your problems much quicker than worrying, stressing and trying to wrestle the problem to the ground.

Chapter 3

The Science of Energy – It's All There Is

*E*verything is energy. This is not just some New Age platitude; it is backed up by the work of scientists and thought leaders, Albert Einstein and Nikola Tesla among them. The earth and everything on it is made of energy, including our bodies and even our thoughts. That said, energy vibrates at different levels — some energy is slower and so it appears denser. For example, a couch is pretty dense; water is less dense, and air is not dense at all. Our thoughts also vibrate at certain frequencies, all of which project out into the Universe. Thoughts of worthiness, for example, vibrates at different frequency than that of unworthiness; the same is true for thoughts of happiness and thoughts of fear. Now, imagine what happens when our thoughts shoot out into the Universe into the whirlpool of energy with everyone's thoughts, all merging into one. An excellent positive example of this is prayer, with both religious texts and scientific studies describing the powerful effects of prayer on healing.

Thoughts are energy going beyond our own field. They project out into a room. Have you ever walked into a room and felt the tension, only to learn that the people there had been arguing before you arrived?

You felt the energy as soon as you entered, though you may have just thought you were "reading" their facial expressions or other body language. The same is true when you meet someone and instantly know if you like them or not. Now, that may change a bit once you get to know them, but their energy gave you a quick clue about them. I've noticed after doing a lot of work to clear my energy (i.e. Reiki attunements) that some people will remark on the change in my energy. I've also noticed that little kids, especially really little ones, look at me and smile more than ever before. I'm sure it helps that I'm a mom, but even that would be an energetic change.

Imagine that you allow a lot of what we'll call "I'm not worthy" thoughts to float through your brain. As mentioned above, each thought has its own vibration, and to make it simple I'm going to compare it to colors. Let's say a positive thought is a beautiful yellow or pink. It's bright and nurturing and feels good. Negative thoughts have a darker color, brown or black, and feel heavy and thick. The lighter thoughts will help lighten your own vibration, and the darker thoughts start to muddy you up. They also, as mentioned before, combine with all the other energy in the Universe. Do you see how you create an impact on the universal energy?

Let's examine how a thought pattern might start to emerge in the Universe. A benign thought like, "I should color my hair brown" goes out. I am thinking that I love brown hair because it's so beautiful and smart-looking, and I'd like to find the perfect shade of brown for me. Suddenly, everywhere I go I notice women with the most gorgeous shades of brown hair. I have placed my focus on something, and the Universe is delivering it in spades.

Let's return now to those "I am not worthy" thoughts. When you think such a thought, it sends its low-energy vibration out into the Universe. Now you have unintentionally shot a negative energy wave out to others. And, as like energy attracts like energy, you are also going to attract to you people whose thoughts are vibrating at that same frequency.

Conversely, if you begin thinking positive thoughts about yourself, they will go out into the Universe and spread that kind of energy. You will attract others of the same frequency to you, which in turn raises your vibration even more. If you've ever heard the saying, "Guard your thoughts" and wondered what it meant, well, this is it. We are all sparks of the divine. Our thoughts shape the reality we live in. That's power. We can be part of a great change, a wonderful new world just by guarding our thoughts and sending out positive energy.

I used to hate driving to work. I would get on interstate and instantly become crabby. I live in North Dakota, so there's not much to complain about in terms of the traffic; however, as an empathic person, I believe I was taking on everyone's negative energy. And, judging from my mood, there seemed to be a lot of it. If we can imagine most people's mornings and the state of things, it's easy to imagine a road full of not-so-happy people. Mornings can be tough. I began to be more intentional about maintaining my energy field, and more importantly, I also started to bless people. Any time someone would cut me off or do something that annoyed me, I would say, "Bless you." Sometimes I had to say it two or three times before I could mean it. The first time, my teeth would clench a little bit. The second time I couldn't stop the eye roll, and by the third time, I nailed it. I said it with meaning and love. Then I got to the point where I would think, *How do I know what kind of day they are having, or what kind of life? Maybe the one thing they could use more than anything is a blessing.*

Energetic or not, it started to help me change the way I saw people. It was less about "me vs. them" and more about "us." I was their advocate now, understanding that life circumstances shape our lives, and sometimes our circumstances give us more darkness than we can overcome. I started to remember that they are a soul first, person second. The least I could do was bless them, provide a little healing and loving energy. And when we understand that everything is energy, our positive thoughts go out like little rays all over interstate (or at the grocery store or gas station) and shed a little bit of light during some stressful times. My small thoughts may have a positive impact on the world. Your every thought creates a reality and here you thought you didn't matter. Well, now you know! Many blessings to you. Namaste.

Words too are energy, and very powerful energy at that. And, like our thoughts, each word holds its own vibration. The phrase "I am," for example, literally shapes your reality, that's why it's so important to mind how we use it. Words have the power to hurt or heal, so try speaking carefully for a while and see how things change for ourselves and those around us. Thinking and speaking deliberately takes practice and staying away from negative thinking can be tricky. It sneaks up on you in ways you don't always expect. That's why it helps to intentionally incorporate positive "I am" statements into your day. If you have trouble coming up with your own, there are a ton of CDs, YouTube videos, and other resources out there that can help.

Some phrases feel good and others don't feel quite as nourishing, but we get in the habit of saying them over and over, all day long. Let's examine the following phrases.

> I want
>
> I will try or I tried
>
> I should
>
> I have to
>
> I choose to
>
> I create
>
> I allow

Which of these phrases feel good to you? Which feel uncomfortable? You are a creator and when you say "I want" it, you give your power away. You can want forever, and you can try forever. Saying "I should" also implies that you are not a sovereign, creator being. Those phrases feel wrong. There is no lack in the Universe unless you believe there is.

When you use phrases like "I create", "I allow" or "I choose to" you take back your power and signal your trust in the Universe. You reclaim your sovereignty as a creator being because you are.

If you need more proof, try it out. Close your eyes and say a negative phrase, such as, "I am ugly." How does that feel in your body? Can you feel it shrink back a little? Now say, "I am beautiful; I am worthy." Can you feel the difference? Say it a few times and if you don't believe it, don't worry. Just pretend, and with time and practice you will own it as your truth. You will feel the truth of it in your body. Remember, everything you say is, in fact, an affirmation. You are giving your order, your command to the Universe, stating your intention. It comes down to caring enough about yourself to choose the words that make you feel good while leaving the rest. It's deciding you matter enough. When I find myself slipping into old patterns, I simply make a different choice. It's okay to have patience with ourselves, keeping in mind that it's all about the journey.

Each day of this journey presents us with opportunities to learn; however, how we view these opportunities — for examples, as "lessons" or "mistakes" — has a great impact on our souls. When I was a reporter and did a story or, even worse, a live shot, I almost couldn't watch them because I was sure they were terrible. I would agonize over them, critical of every "um" or pause or misspoken word I thought I'd said. Then I would gather up my courage and watch them and realize with a sense of relief that they weren't bad at all. The mistakes I'd imagined weren't even there. How often, I wonder, do we blow our perceived shortcomings out of proportion? If we could only have the true image, the objective image of ourselves to look at, maybe our hearts and minds could rest a little easier. And maybe in place of the "video" we say to our angels, help me with this one, it's a burden. If we can do that, our angels can be the mirror to the truth of our soul's beauty. Maybe we can see ALL our experiences as lessons, rather than life sentences. Because when we lift that off our backs, we can travel our path that much easier, allowing us to be the light we are truly meant to be.

Rewrite Your Story

One night, my husband and I were having a conversation and he said, "Well, I'm just not wired that way. I'm not like you; I can't relax. I have to keep moving." Except that's not the truth, not really. It's just the story he's been telling himself for years. There is no fault here; his story very closely mirrored that of his father, while my story mirrored very closely that of my own dad. Furthermore, I believe these are the sorts of choices we made for our lives before incarnating here, which is why we chose the families we did in the first place. They are part of the lessons we chose to experience for our soul's growth. That said, we can rewrite our story. I believe it's what we came here to do. The power is ours.

What narrative do you rely on to shape or explain who you are? Did you know you can begin to change it any time you'd like? There's a saying: perception is reality. What words do you use to describe yourself, your life? Are you tired, busy, getting old, too this or too that? Do you perceive your life as good, bad, gruesome? Does your body "fall apart" when you turn forty? With every thought, word or idea, we build our life's narrative. And, as in the case with my husband and myself, these narratives started not with us, but with the people who cared about us the most, the ones who raised us. They fed us ideas and truths constantly. It was all very well-intentioned, meant to give us a realistic view, to protect us, to educate us. It's important for us to start to observe our beliefs, our thoughts and our words. One way is to begin journaling about it until you have an accurate picture of your narrative. And remember, there's no need to judge it. It's just a thought, just a belief, and it's completely benign. Even the thoughts you think are "evil" I would argue are simply thoughts that can be sent away on a beautiful cloud to be cleared or transmuted. Comb through your thoughts, then take each one that no longer serves you, lift it up and release it to the light. This will be a lifelong process.

Now that you're aware of your narrative, how do you change it? There are lots of ways and it simply becomes finding what works best for you. One place to start might be back with those kids.

Young children don't have stories. They take the path of least resistance and flow with the current. They have fun. In fact, the only time they stop is when adults muck it all up, right? Now, let's try writing our story from the perspective of our inner child. Grab a pen and a lot of paper and think about what you would like your story to look like. Make it a good one, an ice cream all the time, recess 24-7 kind of story. Don't worry about what you're writing, just have fun and don't quit until you've run out of ink or your heart tells you to stop. Then go back and read what you wrote and see how it turned out. See what truths you told yourself. How does your new story feel?

Ask yourself what gets in the way of taking a child's approach to writing or rewriting your story. You'll probably find that the biggest culprit is fear. As the saying goes, though, "Fear is false evidence appearing real."

Aside from the appropriately timed flight or fight response, that analogy is pretty accurate. Most of the time, our fears don't pan out to be much or anything at all, just as our perceived shortcomings (i.e. my belief that my interviews were terrible) turn out to be erroneous. This is why we must push past the fear and have faith that we indeed have the power to rewrite the story we would like to manifest in our external reality.

Like our fear, many of our beliefs and even our criticisms of others are also based on misinformation or false evidence. If we could see inside a person's heart, I believe we would find a greater truth as to why he or she is acting the way they do. And with that truth, we would find compassion for their journey. In other words, instead of wondering what is wrong with that person, we might realize that behind the fear or pain or anger they are more like us than we may have previously thought (or maybe more than we want to admit). We might begin to appreciate and have empathy around their journey. We might realize that the truth is not as black and white as we once thought.

What is truth?

Have you thought about where your beliefs come from? Do you question why you believe the things you do, where they originated? A person is a staunch democrat or a republican but why? It's not typically because they've spent a lot of time researching the fundamentals of one party versus another. Usually the person's dad and/or mom is one or the other, and you internalize their political opinions. The same can be said for everything from religion to car brands and even trivial things like dish soap.

Mark Twain once wrote, "Travel is fatal to prejudice, bigotry and narrow mindedness, and many of our people need it sorely on these accounts. Broad, wholesome charitable views of men and things cannot be acquired by vegetating in one little corner of the earth all one's life."

Twain makes a strong statement about the validity of traveling outside our own backyard. If we never live outside of our environment, never question our own set of beliefs, never ask someone about theirs, how can we know ours are right? Have you ever found someone with a completely different set of beliefs and asked them questions? I am talking about asking questions so you can learn, not so you can try to save them or make them understand why your beliefs are better. A local speaker once said we need to exercise our right to be offended. And I believe there is truth to that.

Again, what is truth? There was an image on social media with two people on opposite sides of what appears to be the number nine. Of course, it's only a nine on one side, from the other side, it's a six. It's a lighthearted way to talk about a challenge that can at times create a very real divide among us. How do we see an issue, challenge or belief? How do we see life? Have you ever stopped to question what perspective, bias, belief system you bring into the mix? How it clears or clouds your judgment? I am not necessarily suggesting you change it, but simply understand where it came from and why someone might look at it differently. Why does the person opposite me see a six when it's most definitely a nine? What is truth? And how do we come to our own truth? If we had spent our lives on a different path, would our truth be the same? Can we allow others to walk their own path, gathering their own truth without judgment, holding them in love?

It's important for us to walk our own path getting the answers to our own questions, finding our own truth and allowing that truth to evolve.

We are all looking through a kaleidoscope; however, we tend to look through it, set it into place and never move it. We think our view through the scope is the only one that's right, and we miss out on so much beauty. It's okay and, I dare say, vital to simply unlock and adjust.

Chapter 4

Watch Your Vibe

*L*et's return to discussing energy, and the vibration we are putting out into the Universe. You must be in vibrational alignment with what you want to manifest or create. Remember, when you think positively about things and are happy, you place yourself in alignment with the higher vibrational things you are trying to attract. When you are in a place of fear, you are not in a place to receive what you desire.

Let's say you go to a restaurant you've been wanting to try. You are seated at a wonderful table on the top floor, and when you look at the menu you are very excited and happy to see that it has all your favorite dishes. The server takes your order, then goes to tend to her other customers. Some time passes, and there is no sign of her or your food. You tell yourself to be patient, but when even more time passes you start to wonder what's going on. All around you, you see others eating and wonder why they have already been served. When your food still doesn't come, you leave the table and head down to the lower floor to look for the server. You have moved out of trust and into fear and doubt. *When is it coming; is it even coming at all? Others are getting their food, why am I not getting mine?* Finally, you give up and return to your table, only to find the meal there waiting for you all along.

How does that metaphor translate to real life? The food order you placed was like the orders you place into the Universe. You put it out there, but then you must have faith that it will arrive. When you insert fear, anger or doubt into the process, when you go to the "lower floor" as in the restaurant example above, you are no longer in a vibrational place to receive. It is only once we raise our energy and return to the location (aka energetic level) where we placed our order, that we realize it has already been fulfilled, in divine timing.

We are always attracting something, whether we realize it or not. We place orders, and the Universe responds in a way that is a match to our vibration. If we are focused on negative emotions or complaining, we simply cannot attract the high vibrational things we desire. We always attract what we believe we deserve. Sometimes those beliefs are unconscious. We may be consciously saying we deserve one thing or another (or trying to convince ourselves as such), but if deep down we hold a different belief (i.e. "Life is hard for me" or "I have to work around the clock to make ends meet." "Money is the root of all evil."), we will draw evidence of this into our life. The Universe wants to give us what we want and uses our words plus our feelings or desires to do so. If you want more money but believe it's the root of all evil, the Universe will respond by keeping "evil" or money away.

On the other hand, if we focus on the act of feeling good first, then all the good things we've ordered will be on the "same floor," the same vibration as we are. We will be an energetic match. We all know those annoying people who, no matter what happens to them, remain calm, even happy. Those people for whom things always seem to work out. This is not luck nor a series of coincidences; it's their attitude, their positive thinking and their ability to stay in that feeling of joy. It's their vibration and belief in what they deserve that causes them to attract more of what they want and less of what they don't want. They expect good things – either because they were taught to by their parents or adopted it themselves. And when something bad does happen, they use this "contrast" between what they desire and what they see in their reality as a resource. They use the contrast to guide them back onto the path to what they want, namely, by placing their focus on the things that show up in their life with positivity and gratitude. They focus on their happiness, and since they believe they deserve it, they will always find their way back to it.

Whether we realize it or not, being on that path is our natural state. The Universe, or our guardian angels, or whatever you prefer to call divine assistance is always providing clues and messages to guide us to what makes us feel good and what makes life feel more fulfilling. Sometimes we forget to pay attention to the signs we are given. Sometimes we block the messages altogether, with our own thoughts, actions or beliefs. When we put any little doubt in the Universe, we block the signal before it has a chance to come back to us.

If we are aligned with what we want to attract and powerfully excited by it, it has no choice but to become our reality. Let's say you fall into the lake. The first thing you do is try to fight. You flail your arms and kick your legs, but the harder you fight, the more you sink. You start to panic and realize you don't even know how to find your way to the top anymore. It is a losing battle…

The minute you stop fighting, and the minute you relax, you rise up. Your face feels the fresh air, your lungs fill with oxygen and, if you can really relax, you'll float on top of the water. We make our way, not by fighting, but by relaxing into it and allowing ourselves to flow with the energy of the water. We are so trained to fight. And historically speaking, we've often needed to. But the world has changed drastically from when our ancestors ran from tigers, and it continues to evolve. These are no longer the times of constant fight or flight; these are the times for allowing and receiving.

The ability to create or manifest exactly what we want is greater than it's ever been, but only if we can get into that receptive state. If we can just trust and notice what's working, we can create space for our most desired life to unfold. When we relax, allow and let the Universe speak to us, we use our creativity and go with the flow. We are using our feminine side to listen to that inspiration; we use the masculine side, not to push or fight, but to do what we are inspired to do. That is balance.

The Long Haul: Enjoying Life with Patience and Trust

Like anything else, it tends to take a little time to see the results from the work we do. That doesn't mean it's not working. I don't know how many times I've started an exercise plan, only to give up just when it was starting to work. I'd start the plan with the goal of losing ten or twenty pounds. I'd look at my diet and start eating a little better. I'd add in exercise and really stick with it, making sure I headed to the gym or got on the treadmill three to five times a week. Then, after a couple weeks or a month, maybe longer, I would get discouraged because it didn't seem to be working and go back to a life of junk food and leisure.

Here is the funny thing. After a while, I would suddenly notice that my pants were getting tight again…except, I'd never noticed that they were loosening up! Hmmm. That's when I realized I had given up just when it was starting to work and, had I been patient, I would have seen noticeable results. Instead, I was right back at the beginning. I thought about how much progress I would have made if I had just stuck with it.

We start an exercise regimen with the intention to get healthier and stronger. And though we don't like to think about how long it might take, we know we can't sit on the couch thinking about exercise and expect our muscles to get stronger or our body to get leaner. And we don't work out once and expect the number on the scale to change (though that would be nice!). What we do expect is that we will start a journey of good health. We focus on the number of reps we can do and the cardio that makes our heart rate go up and sweat collect on our brow. We don't look at our arm and say, where is the muscle?!? We don't throw a tantrum and say, "I quit, that didn't work." We know that eventually, if we keep doing the reps and the cardio, our body will reflect the time we spent. It happens slowly, and we might not even notice the changes (except for those willing to take a photo at the beginning). As we continue, we slowly get stronger; we quietly reach and surpass our goals. When we stick with it, a long-term, regular routine shows us results. Oftentimes, without our even realizing it, we actually start to like to exercise. We like how we feel when we do it, and how it makes us feel overall. It becomes an ally. It supports us, as all friends do.

It's the same thing with this work. You do the inner work and focus on the doing, and slowly you start to feel better…and better…and better. Things start going your way, however, just like with my pants, the improvement can be so subtle that it's easy to miss…until you stop. Then in a short time, things revert back to the way they were before you shifted your life. The synchronicities stop, your mood might be a little lower, stress might get to you again. But this is good news. Yes, I said it: *good news*. Why? Because this is simply contrast, sending a clear reminder to us about what we want and what we don't. Once we remember what we don't want, we can focus again on the things that bring us to what we do want. And once we know what to do, it's easy to invite our allies back into our lives. Just like working out, it can be frustrating to realize we'd given up just as we were seeing results. Yet this too is a lesson. We learn to stick with it. We know it works. We realize that we can see change and that it doesn't even take that long. Also, just like working out, the contrast teaches us that it's a lifestyle change, not just a quick fix. In time, the work we are doing, the meditation or affirmations become a welcome and integral part of our lives. It starts to make sense, and it even becomes fun!

All this work on ourselves goes back to our secret garden. It's important to prune, tend to and love the garden so it can really flourish. Sometimes we don't know exactly what we are doing, and it shows. Take, for example, my vegetable garden — my real one. From year to year, my tomato plants have yielded very different harvests. One summer there were so many tomatoes packed in a little space, it was hard to find them. I was digging, reaching turning this way and that trying to get out every red bite of heaven. I was always missing some and would find them too late. The next year, I had some sort of root rot thing. Every tomato would get to be a certain size and then the bottom would turn black and yucky — boo! The next year, I put them in pots, but they didn't grow. At all. It was more than a little disappointing to put all that work into the little guys and wind up with no veggies, but it was also an important part of learning and understanding what works and what doesn't. It taught me to be patient with the process.

If life were easy to figure out, we wouldn't want to be here because it would be boring. The contrast is what keeps us entertained and spurs our growth. But soon, we start to get little pieces figured out. We learn why the bottom of the tomatoes get black, or why putting them in a pot doesn't work; we learn how to make one small change or another to get a different result. Before we know it, we are growing perfect tomatoes year after year, and we look back at our toils with appreciation for how much we learned. And when someone asks how we grow such juicy, delicious tomatoes, we have wisdom to share because we've walked that path and we know. And isn't it fun to share your knowledge with others? It's what makes our circles strong. Which brings me to another important point — we too can learn to ask for help along the way. While it's true all the answers are within us, we can always learn from the experience of others. They might not have all the answers, or the right answers for you (back to trusting our own knowing); however, their knowledge can make the road a little easier to travel, and in many cases a lot more fun!

That said, while it's great to learn and to begin to work through what we don't know, it's also important to focus on and develop our strengths. Why spend so much time trying to fix what isn't "good enough" when we could spend our time building upon what is already working? I learned this lesson during an intuitive class, where trust in one's ability is absolutely essential. Sometimes this is easier said than done, especially when you're working on something that often doesn't provide immediate evidence. As we went through some exercises to strengthen our intuition, the instructor emphasized over and over: "Follow the hits, follow the hits. Don't worry about the ones you didn't get right." It was some of the best advice I've ever received.

Focusing on the hits is truly a lesson that we could weave throughout our lives. The question is, how do we move from focusing on what needs fixing to leaning into what we already do well and brings us joy? Well, for one, it might help to learn to relax.

Relax, Step One

What does your day look like? How much time do you carve out to simply relax? If you haven't done that in a while, now might be a good time to start (and, honestly, scrolling through Facebook really doesn't count as relaxing). Like the other steps in this book, start slowly, perhaps with just five minutes. If you're thinking you don't have five minutes, consider what you do in a day. Can you find five minutes at the beginning of the day, or maybe over lunch? Can you briefly pause that show you're bingeing on Netflix? You see my point — no matter how busy we are, we all can reallocate five minutes to simply being quiet. You'll soon find yourself craving this time to yourself and finding ways to set aside even more of it.

When we learn to be still, breathe deeply from our belly and allow ourselves a moment to just be, our heart has space to begin to reveal a little bit of our path. By quieting the chatter in our mind, we release any resistance, and we can begin to hear what our soul has been waiting to say. At first your soul may be very quiet, maybe a little timid, but if you nurture it and offer it quiet acceptance, it will become louder. If you've ever dipped your feet in a lake, you know that if you hold very still little fish will come closer to you, eventually getting close enough to nibble on your toe. That inner voice is the same way – get quiet, stop splashing around, and it will reveal itself to be our best friend, our heart, our higher self.

Our heart holds all the power. It drives our creativity, our ideas and our peace. We think our ideas start in our mind, but they start in our heart and travel to our mind. Our heart and soul are the sun to our inner garden. And when we get quiet, it has space to breathe, space to find its voice. And we can allow it to take center stage and spend time with that inner child, doing whatever it wants to do, draw, write, dance, walk in nature or sing. Just give it a chance, allow and create and don't worry about or judge the result. It doesn't matter what your dancing, art or singing looks like to anyone else. In time, we will once again remember our wholeness; we will begin to enjoy heaven on earth. Because heaven is inside us. It always was. We've always been wearing the ruby slippers, we just forgot to look down at our feet.

I invite you to write down all the things you would want from a best friend. How would you treat them and how would you want them to treat you? What words would you say to them, what kind of advice would you give them? Do this each night for a week. First, write a paragraph or two about how you are feeling, what you did, what you are struggling with et cetera, then write an answer to yourself as your best friend, offering yourself encouragement, honest advice, and feedback. Then go back and read the entries and see what you learned. It takes practice to become our own best friend. Most of all, it takes patience, just as we would expect from a friend.

Chapter 5

Time for Women to Rise

*Y*ou can change the world, or you can let the world change you. You can't have it both ways. You can be led by fear or love. You must choose. And even if you don't make a decision, you are still choosing. You are choosing a default mode — ego control — and that's probably not what you want, yet you've been doing it as long as you can remember. It's time to stop, but first we have to ask why we've been staying small, why we've been holding our breath rather than taking in all life has to offer. That answer can be found in a quick internet search.

Human history is filled with stories of strong women repressed by a system designed to keep their true powers from making a difference. These stories go back to the caveman days and, though things have improved, it continues today. One of the most profound stories occurred during the time of Jesus. What is the first thing you think of when you hear the name Mary Magdalene? If you grew up in any of the Christian denominations, probably nothing flattering, as for centuries she was denounced as a prostitute, an unclean woman. In recent years, we are discovering a very different, very empowering portrait of her, as someone who not only witnessed Jesus' miracles but served as his trusted confidant. Some researchers contend that the powers that be removed parts or added falsehoods to the Bible to bolster a patriarchal society. Yet, for many, those traditional negative beliefs persist.

Take a moment to set aside any beliefs that have been passed down to you. Imagine that Mary Magdalene was a powerful woman who walked beside Jesus. Imagine she was admired and considered an equal among his disciples. How would that change your perception of women throughout history? Would you start to question that history, wondering whether it really represents the truth, or a false system of beliefs? Has history really been altered to degrade and demean women for centuries? And why? Maybe it's because we hold more power than we have allowed ourselves to imagine…or remember. This isn't about judging the past, however, it's about moving forward. Whether you believe history has been accurately written or deviously tampered with, it's time to accept our own potential and the truth of our divinity. Our power is now, right here in this now moment. It's about taking back our right to choose what we believe, and remembering how to trust our inner knowing.

Another famous example of the repression of female power is the assault on "witches." History is full of stories of such women who were hung and burned at the stake for "evil deeds," when the truth is that many served their communities as healers and priestesses. They owned their power and thus were considered a threat. Even today the word witch conjures fear in the hearts of many. Take a moment to ponder what comes up when you say those three terms — "witch," "healer," and "priestess." Does it change how you feel about women's power and potential in the world?

Salem Witch Trials

Unfortunately, the persecution of alleged witches would be carried from Europe to the New World and would become one of the most tragic events of the Colonial period.

In 1692, a handful of young girls from Salem, Massachusetts fell ill with violent fits, contortions and uncontrollable outbursts of screaming. They tried to remedy it with praying, and when that didn't work, they called in a local doctor, who diagnosed them with "bewitchment." Other girls began exhibiting similar symptoms, and fear ripped through the community. Ironically, according to documents, a neighbor secretly used a "witch's cake" to find out the name of the witches hexing the girls. A short time later, three women, including a slave named Tituba and a homeless mother, were accused of witchcraft. After being beaten, Tituba decided to "confess"; she also started naming other women as witches. Eventually more women did the same until the courts were overrun with women accused of witchcraft, including a four-year-old girl. Some men were also accused. Many women confessed to a covenant with the devil — not surprising given the fact that those who maintained their innocence were executed. Eventually public sentiment turned against the trials, but not before many innocent lives were lost. It is said that more than two hundred people were accused and at least twenty-five people died – nineteen were hanged, one was tortured to death, and another four died in prison while awaiting trial. As for those girls who initially displayed such erratic and frightening behavior? A 1976 study published in Science magazine cited ergot, a fungus found in wheat, rye and other cereals, as the culprit. Ergot causes – you guessed it – delusions, vomiting and muscle spasms. The term "witch hunt" is commonly used to describe an unfair persecution. Yet the negative stereotypes of witches – and women – persist.

When we consider this brutal history, it's no wonder that as women, we struggle to own our power. And even now, the Wiccan faith very much hides in the shadows. What reaction does the word Wiccan stir in you? Is it curiosity, excitement, or something less than positive? Do you think of a beautiful faith that communes with Mother Earth, that values life and uses herbs to heal? Or, do you think of ritual sacrifices and black magic intended to harm all around? What is the truth, and how many powerful healers have died because of egoic fears? And when we think of the people who tortured and executed all those innocent women, how do we react? We have two options: judge them and condemn them or drop into our hearts and forgive them. We can find that spot where the pain and anger sit and allow the light to penetrate and heal it. We can allow the pain to be a dark rich soil in which we place a seed of understanding and hope. Just as each event in our personal lives has the power to teach, so does each event experienced by the collective, if only we're open to it.

Some oppressive history is much more subtle, for example, the story depicted in *Lark Rise to Candleford,* a BBC series based on an autobiographical novel by Flora Thompson. Set in nineteenth century Oxford, it is the story of a young woman who becomes an apprentice to a postmistress. It was the only post office run by a woman. In one episode, the postmistress decides to run for public office. She never had a chance. They were never going to elect a woman since "they already get bossed around enough." It's a very interesting portrayal of powerful female characters navigating life during this oppressive time. Those women saw what they wanted and went after it, no matter how many hardships they had to face. Now, the postal mistress did not win the election, but certainly her brave efforts stirred little pebbles that changed the course of history. These days, when the prejudices against us are even subtler, it is important that we keep asking questions and pushing for what we truly want, that we keep stirring the waters. We are experiencing an unprecedented and exciting awakening of our true feminine intuitive powers, and it's just the beginning.

There are so many examples of women who didn't let life stop them from fulfilling their heart's desire, whether that was to bring a personal dream to fruition or to save the world in their own way. It's easy to look at these women and think there was something so special about them, to think that the rest of us couldn't possibly emulate them or what they accomplished. It's easy to say they were special, super strong or gifted in some way. But if we were able to ask them in the middle of their quest or endeavor how they felt, I wonder what they would say? How many would say they felt defeated, or that the task before them felt impossible? How many would not have walked that path, had they only known how hard it would be?

Sometimes, we take those first steps of a journey not knowing how messy the middle is going to be. I'd imagine it's a little like cleaning out your closet. You decide you're sick of the clutter and commit to taking everything out, sorting it and giving or throwing away what you don't wear. You go into it with enthusiasm, but by the time you get to the middle of it, you wish you'd never come up with the silly idea. But now you're stuck because you're halfway through, and everything is a total mess. You have no choice but to forge ahead. It's okay, though, because you are further along than you realize and even though it looks like it couldn't be any worse, the mess is actually a sign of progress. And before you know it, you've got an organized closet full of clothes you love (if you're like me, some you forgot you owned), and a pile of stuff you will take to Goodwill so someone can feel beautiful. And you feel good because you stuck with it, cleared out the old and made way for new.

So, who are these women cleaning out their closet of life? They are you and me, forging ahead on the only paths we could take, our own destiny.

A Separate History: Women as Healers

It may take a bit more effort, but you can find a rich history of women throughout time and across the world who used their intuitive and healing powers to change the lives of others.

For example, in Native American cultures, women often served as the shaman, or healer, as the leaders of the tribe recognized their ability to nurture, to birth and intuit what men could not.

Right now you may be thinking, all of this historical information about women is interesting but what good does it do us now? Why should we pay attention to any of it? Well, because over time we've lost, or have been robbed of, our connection to our power, and now it is time to reclaim it, to reclaim our birthright as powerful feminine souls. It is time that history stops repeating itself. I'm tired of the world not knowing my power – and yours. Too many women have suffered needlessly, have been persecuted based on fears. And when you think of the world as energy, that fear is part of our timeline. It's part of the reason female relatives and friends try to keep other women in line. I believe our very cells hold that ancestral memory, the pain of lifetimes of persecution. There is a memory of the healer or psychic being ostracized from the village, yet kept alive because the village members needed her knowledge and healing power. There is a collective pain that results in a subconscious belief that we are not enough or even devious. And more importantly a belief that if we hide our power, we will be safe. We will be part of the "village." But the village and its inhabitants are stronger when we rise up and honor our magnificence. You are magnificent.

There is a simmering, festering sore that tells us we are not good enough or don't deserve. When we can heal that deep wound, release it, and allow the light to penetrate the wound we rise to our divine potential; our hearts will sing because we will remember just how worthy we are. And in rediscovering our worthiness we will find so much power, subtle compassionate power that will spill out onto the world like a beautiful pink river, flowing into all the pain, all the nooks and crannies of this earth. That pink river of love and healing will sow new seeds of compassion and understanding. It's time to understand all of that so we can allow the pain to rise up, to be honored and released. We can heal the fears and insecurities. With that weight gone, we can embrace the dreams we have suppressed for so long.

It's time for the beauty, the nurturing and the creative, intuitive power to take its place in this world, not only to empower women, but to restore much-needed balance between the masculine and feminine energies. Am I suggesting you become a bra-burning, women's lib powerhouse? Am I telling you to march on the streets? No, not unless you want to, unless it fills you up. Then, hell yeah, you march away, sistah! But really, we can simply be good to ourselves, honor ourselves, honor our hearts and do what truly makes us happy. We can begin to take inspired action, for that is what holds the power to transform this world. You are so deserving. You are all you need, and your happiness is what the world needs.

Take a moment right now to get quiet. To drop into your heart. Ask what your heart wants, listen and give her a minute to give you an answer. Do that periodically until you can relax and get quiet enough to hear. Honor whatever comes up, whenever it comes up. For me, it doesn't always come right when I drop into my heart because I think too much about it. But the invitation is there, and my heart will take it and speak to me when I'm ready, when I'm quiet. It usually comes to me in a daydream, and it will catch me off guard (in a good, kick-ass way). Point is, trust your own process. Once she speaks, take your heart's advice and go out into this world and find your bliss. That is what will save this world. You are so, so loved. You are love. You are perfect just as you are right now. You ARE magnificent. Can you believe? Can you pretend until you believe?

Being a Girl...What Does that Mean?

When you think about what it means to be a woman or a girl, what comes to mind?

Is it stereotypical gender roles, such as women make coffee; women answer the phones? My pet peeve is when executive assistants need phone coverage and only email the other women in the office to ask for it. Why does it feel so comfortable to stay in our box? If you think about it, you can actually stay pretty safe in a prison. There's food, shelter and a bed, but it's still a prison, nonetheless. It doesn't take much for a comfort zone to become a cell; the good news is that just like the pebble that gets dislodged, it may only take one small action to create a change that ripples through our life and the lives of others. It begins when we question our patterns. It may start internally, but eventually that internal change impacts what's around us.

What gender stereotypes do you see, and possibly accept, in your daily environment? I remember a comment made by a state legislator where I live. He was being asked about a repeal of a state blue law that kept businesses closed until noon on Sundays. I assume he was trying to be witty when he said that his wife didn't need that half-day, because she had plenty of time to spend his money in the other six and half days of the week. Chuckle, chuckle, wink, wink. Just a good ole boy, telling it like it is…or was, in like 1950! For some women, it was a joke (albeit a lame one); they didn't see the harm. And for them, maybe the box has been perfectly adequate. However, for many of us, the box is no longer acceptable, and neither are the sexist comments designed to keep us in it. This revealed a rift among women; in fact, one woman was actually pretty annoyed that I didn't find the comment harmless. It triggered her, either because I threatened the safety she felt in "the box," or because she felt trapped but didn't know how to get out of it.

Believing there's more out there and not knowing how to get it can be truly terrifying and heartbreaking. But that's the thing – all it takes is simply an intention and a willingness to trust our instincts and follow the breadcrumbs the Universe leaves us. And yes, folks around you might get angry. That's okay. They get to have that reaction. Allow them their process without trying to "save them," because you have no idea what lessons they came here to learn. Instead, focus on you and take a step. It's that simple. Trust and take action, trust and take action, over and over again, until you have arrived at your destination. Of course, that will reveal a new, even better destination, and so the journey begins again. It can be filled with laughter and beauty, or it can be something less than that. The choice is always yours.

Chapter 6

Being an Example

"We all come to understand that there is no such thing as a neutral exchange. You leave someone either a little better or a little worse. The best among us, leave others a little better with every nod, every inflection, every interface."

– Dale Carnegie

Not too many of us want to be known as the person who is always telling others what they should have said or done. And most of us don't want to be around a person who does that either. We've probably all been in a situation like that. We say or do something we know was not very nice and the lark next to us makes sure to point it out. At that point, it's pretty easy to get defensive because we already knew whatever we said or did was rude or mean. It may just be easier all around to lead by example. And sometimes we do just that, and we pleasantly surprise ourselves. Other times we don't, and we have just provided ourselves with another learning experience.

I was waiting in line at Dairy Queen one day and an older gentleman in front of me was trying to order. He walked up and the young woman working at the counter asked what he wanted.

"What'dya got?" he asked.

She sighed and with an annoyed look on her face told him they had ice cream. Not satisfied with this answer, he asked what else they had to eat. She started to impatiently rattle off various foods, and when she got to hot dogs, he said that sounded good, he'd take three. He then reached into his wallet and pulled out a checkbook.

"We don't take checks," she said in a flat voice, and the man, now just as annoyed as she, started to walk away.

I paused, taking a moment to let the whole incident sink in. I could have let him walk away. I could have gently lectured the young woman on her lack of customer service. I guess I could have called her manager. She certainly didn't look at the stranger as a friend or as another loving soul deserving of respect and kindness. Of course, I also could have done nothing. I had two kids to wrangle, and it's amazing I had it together enough to even notice the exchange. But I suddenly found myself smiling at the man and saying, "Sir, could I buy you dinner?"

He looked at me, a little confused, so I repeated the offer.

"Well, they don't take checks…"

"Don't worry," I said, "I have a card. What would you like?"

I then ordered him three hot dogs and ordered my kids their meals. He asked my name, and we had a very nice conversation. He told me about his many grandkids and great-grandkids, and that he would have to buy my meal the next time he saw me at Dairy Queen.

As he took his three hot dogs and he left, it dawned on me that I had probably done more for the young woman behind the counter than for him, and that being an example of kindness was far more effective than even the most tactful advice. When we show compassion for others, or for ourselves, we also help those who witness that compassion. We become a light for this world. Honestly, I don't know what the Dairy Queen employee walked away with, and that's okay. We don't need to be attached to outcomes; it is simply about being the wayshower. Ultimately, I think I benefited the most because when we give love freely, it comes back to us in spades. All in all, a good day and really, that's all we can ask for.

And I Meet a Teacher...

I was in line at a local store, waiting behind a middle-aged woman. As I stood there, one judgement-filled thought after another ran through my head – how she stood, how she was talking. I had no reason to judge her and, honestly, I hadn't put much thought into it. I simply didn't check my thoughts. I stepped up to the register, and the store clerk asked if I had any coupons. I said no because I never have coupons. The woman turned around and said, "Oh, do you want a coupon? Here's two." She then handed me two twenty percent off coupons that saved me thirty-eight dollars and hurried off. I watched her walk away, filled with guilt. Here I had been judging her, and she had given me an unexpected gift. She had also led by example; however, instead of learning the lesson of non-judgement, I turned the judgement onto myself. Who was I to think those things about her when I had no idea who she was, or what she might be battling? And since when am I one to judge how someone acts or looks? Then I realized that I should show myself the same compassion I should have shown her. I let it go and forgave myself. I recognized it for the teaching moment that it was, and I sent her gratitude, not so much for the coupons (although that was awesome) but for teaching me to love others without reservation and to forgive myself when I don't.

Think of a time when someone acted as an example for you. Do you tend to place such people on a pedestal, as though they are better than you? Well…don't. Chances are those you admire, who act as anchors in the storm, aren't much different from you (meaning you've been the anchor many times, for many people, without even realizing it). If we can figure out our own stuff, deal with our own insecurities and really shine, we become a beautiful lighthouse in this storm of life. Just our actions, our smile, our happiness can become a beacon, calling others home to their own heart. That is what the world needs.

When my son was about seven, he was so kind and so good at so many things. But like a lot of kids his age (and, I dare say, many adults), he found saying sorry quite difficult. It was like admitting defeat. I would try to explain that saying sorry was more like saying "I love you" than saying "I'm wrong" or "I surrender," though to be honest it never really sunk in. When people make conflict about their ego, it becomes about that instead of the thing that actually happened (or how to move beyond whatever happened). On the other hand, when we take the high road, even when we believe we are in the right, we have the potential to resolve conflict in a healthy, healing way. Of course it's important to maintain healthy boundaries by not letting people hurt you or take advantage of you. You can forgive and maintain boundaries. Even better, if we can forgive and release the burden of a grudge or hurt, we lighten our load and heal ourselves. I invite you to have a forgiving heart, remembering that if someone could do better, they would.

Chapter 7

Others' Light, Your Heart

*B*ack when I was working as a marketing professional, a coworker was offered a high-level communications position at local company. It was a pretty good gig, and while I was happy for her, I couldn't help but wonder why she had gotten it. She had a background in communications, but not a long history, and it wasn't what she was doing in her current position. In fact, her new job was more aligned with what I was doing. Basically, I was jealous that I hadn't been offered something so fancy-sounding and felt I was qualified for. Now, would I have taken the job? No, I had other irons in the fire, yet it still felt like a blow. I allowed it to be a sign from the Universe that I was not worthy. It didn't matter that it was not at all what I wanted and that things I truly did want were flowing my way. I decided that her success was somehow indicative that I was lacking.

This is something most of us have done at one point or another – we look at someone else and wonder what makes them so special. Or worse, we come up with reasons why they are not special at all and therefore undeserving of whatever blessing they have received. We say things like, "Who does she think she is anyway? I could lead this group, do that project, manage that person much more effectively." The question is, if our hearts were truly full, would we need to compare ourselves to others in that way? Of course not. On the other hand, if we caught ourselves and stopped thinking and speaking that way, wouldn't we have more space to fill our hearts with the things that truly matter? Of course we would. What would happen if we sat with our fear of failure, or being left out or left behind, while at the same time honoring another's success? Imagine how liberating it would be to say, "She deserves this and I'm excited for her. She deserves that opportunity and I deserve _____ (go on, fill in the blank.)"

How often do you compare yourself to others in big or small ways? (Hint - every time you feel that twinge of jealousy or ask, "Why does she/he always get the good breaks?" and so on.) When you think or speak this way, you are actually blocking what your own heart is trying to tell you; however, when you start listening to your heart, become fully present in your own life, and do what makes you feel alive and fulfilled, that's when you will truly be able rejoice in others' blessings. If you're not there yet, don't judge yourself, just recognize your feelings as a sign of an imbalance and an opportunity to heal. If you can sit with feelings of envy, rather than trying to bury them, you will eventually be able to breathe and feel through and release them. You can free yourself.

So, how do you work through something like that, and what do I mean by "feel it out"? There are many ways, but one way is to acknowledge the feeling and let it come up. Ask your head to step aside and let your heart guide you. You may want to try automatic writing, which sounds very "advanced" but is basically just writing whatever comes to you without judgement. Eventually, you will pour out what's in your heart, what you long for. You'll write down the hurts you've been carrying or the anger that's been holed up deep down in your subconscious. You can let it all come out without judgement. They are just thoughts, and we don't have to own them. We can release them.

Once you are done journaling, you may want to burn it, which is a very powerful way to release all the energy. You may want to cry and that's a good thing. Crying is healthy and effective, your body's way of purging all that emotion. Imagine each tear is a sweet little angel carrying your pain and sorrow up to heaven to be released and transmuted. If you journal and the next day you bawl your eyes out, know that you've just done some very good, healing work. Just allow yourself to be curious about life and let each feeling act as a guide.

Our emotions are valuable – ALL of them. We shame them like we shame our bodies or like we shame people for not thinking, acting or behaving as we do. But really, our emotions are simply us, talking to ourselves. They are saying, "Hey, look at me; I'd like to communicate with you."

We all have inner demons. And if we take a moment to get quiet, we allow some of them to come up so they can be released for good. What do you struggle with? What makes you shrink into yourself when you think about it? Inner demons can be simple or so complex it takes you much inner work to understand them and start to face them. It's not meant to be a quick process. It's a journey, and journeys are beautiful. Journeys are even better when we take our time and really experience them. Once we start to face our demons and heal them, we realize that each one is a fear created by a misconception or a belief that is not true.

I came up against some of these false beliefs while writing this book, one in particular during an online writing class. The organizer brought in a successful author who spoke about the process of marketing our book and getting it out to people who want it. She talked about how the publishing industry has changed and now it's up to the author to market their own book.

As I listened to her and other participants excitedly ask questions about the process, my stomach started to turn a little. Who, I wondered, would want to read anything I had to say? It's a book for women, but women don't really like me. How was this going to work?

As they spoke, I started to make to-do lists, busy work to distract me from the real issue. I knew that I was going to need to break through my fears and barriers if I was ever going to be brave enough to market this book. I realized that despite my fears, I knew this book might help someone break through their own barriers that were keeping them from their fullest potential and keeping their beautiful gifts from the world. That first woman, I decided, would be me. Because, despite all my fears, I do want to be a well-known author, and I am one of those weirdos who likes to speak in front of people. It's a rush, it's fun, and – if I could allow myself a moment of pride – I can be pretty good at it. First, though, I would have to understand where those fears originated so I could move past them and onto a different truth. A truth where I CAN believe that someone might just want to hear what I have to say. That class brought plenty of realizations, and since then I've done the work to dig deeper into my heart and uncover a little more of my garden waiting to bloom and to flourish.

Fear is a powerful motivator. It can save us when we are in physical danger by igniting the fight or flight response. However, it can also hinder us, especially when no actual threat exists. A common reaction to fear, for example, when we want to make a decision or move forward with a new "thing," is to become frozen in place. In fact, many of us tend to retreat from the situation or idea entirely. But what if we were to shift our perspective around fear? What if we were able to recognize it as a teacher?

Get quiet and sit with your fear for a moment; allow it to reveal more about why it is there. From this vantage point, it is much easier to see fear as False Evidence Appearing Real. We can't block fear out entirely; however, we can recognize it as a signal that we're getting to something real. Then, with this new understanding, return to your present situation and make a tiny decision to move forward, to not let the fear paralyze you. Just focus on that one thing and leave the big picture worrying for another day. When you accomplish that one thing, celebrate your accomplishment and enjoy the moment before moving on to the next. If you get stuck, close your eyes and say to yourself and to the Universe, "I'm stuck, I invite help, I invite inspiration." Then get quiet or move on to something else and trust that the answer will come in its time.

We all have fears, but if we let our fears stop us, we keep our gifts from the world. Someone needs what you offer, so don't keep it hidden. It's not fair to them, and it's not fair to you. Sometimes it helps to visualize the person you are helping. Maybe it's a photo of someone you really care about, such as a family member or friend. Maybe it's an image of someone with whom you could see yourself being friends, or someone representing the women who could benefit from your gifts. It may even be a picture of you, to signify that you are fulfilling your own heart's desire by sharing your gifts. You can place their picture on your desk or someplace else you are sure to see it in order to remind you of what you are doing and why. It will help you shift from thinking about this from a "me perspective" to a "helping others" perspective, and those around you will benefit from your new energy and light. And when you do start to become afraid, remember that fear is a door, and it will open to your most blessed life.

When I was younger, I was somewhat shy and quiet; I always just blended in. Even though I was a reporter, in a position where I should have felt popular and –I don't know– "fancy," I felt like I was a dime-a-dozen. I felt forgettable, average, and that was sort of okay. It was comfortable, safe. This may be because I believed that when you're above average, when you start to stand out from the crowd, you can be criticized. The spotlight is on you, and everyone can see you and all your flaws. You are no longer safe.

When we look at who we are and who we want to be, it's important to be honest about what holds us back. In attempting to stay safe, I had chosen to blend in and become part of the wallpaper. I didn't hurt anyone because I didn't outshine them. I was pretty but not too pretty, smart but not too smart. The only way I knew to lift others up (and maybe not to feel their pain) was to back up into the shadows as much as I could. I had fun, sometimes a little too much fun but always remaining within what I considered the safety zone. My actions were always in line with what I was supposed to do and be.

As I began to work on remembering who I am and uncover my light, I started listening to affirmations (usually on my way to work). One of these affirmations – "Taking risks is the path to growth" – particularly resonated with me. As we sit in our sameness and our safeness – our refusal to stand out – what are we giving up? What are we not allowing in our lives? We are safely tucked in the middle, but what's out there on the edge? What vast beautiful landscape of potential are we missing? When we realize our safety is also what prevents our growth, it becomes time to step a little closer to the edge. And isn't it true that powerful events, "good" or "bad," provide us the most incredible growth? For it's when we step to the edge that we learn were always meant to fly.

And, sure, we all face our own self-doubt when we step to the edge. We tend to think our self-doubt is something new or unique to us. Would it surprise you to know how much self-doubt I felt writing this book? Like a ninja warrior, stealth and silent, the fear crept in so quietly at first that I didn't even know it was in the room. Sitting at my desk, dreaming, planning (and perhaps overconfidently) typing away toward my daily word count, I never saw her coming. I thought I had kicked her out for good. I thought I was a new person, bravely conquering a new world.

Then, suddenly, I realized I was doing everything *but* writing. I was too busy to make it a priority, too tired or too this or too that. But really, I wasn't too anything. It was her, a figure dressed in black, quietly staring me down from the corner of the room. At least that's how

I imagine fear to be. Her pointy finger and deep penetrating laugh remind you of what she really thinks of your idea, whatever it is. It can be enough to send you running. You know she's there when you find yourself cleaning that closet or doing some other task you would normally never do, anything to distract you from the fear of the failure or the fear of success. However, if you can learn to sit with the fear and understand her, you will realize the truth: that self-doubt and the internal critical voice get louder the closer you get to the real, earthmoving wow stuff. Fear is an indication you are onto something big. It's your ego trying to keep you safe, and that's okay. But there's a point when the ego (fear) needs to get out of your damn way, and you need to stop cleaning the closet and get back to work.

As I type, I know that I'm moving forward, one word at a time, trusting the process and letting myself stay open to it. You don't have fight or struggle, just be present and open and allow it to flow through you. Allow it to become whatever it's meant to be. When we simply begin to work the puzzle, putting one piece in place at a time, eventually we start to see the bigger picture. We see something much better than we could have ever imagined. I believe that's why we can't see the big picture or the full puzzle at first, because what we would envision is not nearly big enough. Spirit sees so much more potential. Spirit sees how great we are and how powerful we are. We just don't always dream as big as our true potential.

Stop and ask yourself, what do you really think of yourself? Do you think you are just some average person with no specialness, no noteworthy attributes? If so, you couldn't be more wrong. If you think you are anything less than divine, you have a gross misconception of your own soul's value. There is something inside you so magnificent that if you could see it you would find it blindingly, breathtakingly beautiful. It would be so overpowering, so bright that you'd probably need to turn away or close your eyes until they could adjust to the brightness. You may not recognize yourself at first and then the tears may come as you start to remember the vast, immeasurable beauty you hold when you recognize the soul you truly are. You are nothing less than pure light, pure beauty, and pure love. You are a divine spark of the Creator. You need nothing and no one to make you whole. You have always been this. You've just forgotten, and remembering is part of your journey, and now is the time. The dawn is breaking.

You are light, here to shine for the world. Have faith in that. It's time to let it sink in for good. You are a candle that is forever lit. Say this as loudly as you feel comfortable. "I am a divine light that is forever lit. I am magnificent." I dare you to scream and holler it out from your front step! That ought to get the neighbors talking.

Get Excited

Excitement is a sign that whatever you are doing is the right path. Ever notice that when you're on a fun vacation you never get fatigued? You run around all day, exploring, swimming, sunbathing or whatever, then fall into a peaceful sleep at the end of the day. The next morning, you wake full of enthusiasm, excited to do it all over again. Where does all this energy come from? When you think about it, many of the tasks you do on a normal day aren't that much more taxing but, man, they sure are tiring. The fatigue you feel on those days is a sign of resistance.

When you are doing the things you love, that are soul-driven, you have boundless energy. You might still be busy from morning until night, but it's inspired action, exciting. That is how life is supposed to be all the time. It's how life can be if we are brave enough to start making some changes. It doesn't have to happen overnight, and it probably won't. But it can. That is the truth we can all begin to remember, if we want. It's the key to a fulfilling and "vacation-worthy" life.

Others' Light, Your Heart

Have you ever had a job that was so unfulfilling or detrimental to you that on Sunday nights (or maybe every night) you would get a sick feeling in your stomach, dreading the day/week ahead? Ugh, that's the worst place to be. I once worked in an environment that was so toxic and so negative that I went home every night miserable and crying. I didn't understand how to "be a better employee" or how to fit in better. The truth is, I wasn't really doing anything wrong. I certainly made mistakes, but I was willing to work hard and learn. Instead, I felt bullied and marginalized. It was only after I left that I realized what a valuable learning experience this was, a great way to learn about who I was and how I defined my worth. It taught me about who I wanted to be and what I was willing to do to be successful. I learned that I wanted to be part of a team in which everyone was empowered to be their best and no one lied, gossiped or backstabbed to get ahead. And, when I decided I was worthy of a perfect job, I found it.

Sometimes we hover in a negative situation too long because we are afraid of change. Maybe we are afraid of wanting or expecting something bigger or better, that we will find out that we're not worthy. But that's not true. We are worthy. The only thing standing in our way is our own belief in what we deserve. It can also be easy to lose trust in the process, even for those of us who believe in divine guidance and protection. Why can we believe our guardian angels can keep us from getting hit by busses and other horrible things, but not that they can guide us to the job that would give us the most joy? If we can remember that there is no bad path, no wrong turns and no mistakes, we will have the freedom to take a risk and make a bold choice. Doesn't that excite you?

Chapter 8

Go Easy, Love!

It's all a beautiful process.

One morning my son became really upset when my husband slipped out of the house without him. My son was sad that he didn't get to go along to the bagel store. I told him someday he'd be able to drive, and he could slip out without his dad. That turned his tears into laughter as he danced around, thinking about taking the car and driving away on his own. He didn't sit down and start to fret about the when and how or cry about how he couldn't drive yet. He knew he couldn't drive because he hadn't learned enough, his body wasn't big enough. When it was time, he would be ready.

While we don't always see our path so clearly laid out, the truth is that when we are ready for the next step, it will be obvious. It always is, isn't it? The next step tends to call us, beckon us on when it's the perfect time. If you think back to some of the decisions, big or small, that you've made, you may recall, despite maybe a little nervousness or fear, you also had a sense of knowing. There was a certainty deep in your soul, quietly and gently pressing you on. And sometimes you ignored it and the thing went away; other times it happened anyway. Maybe it's a job in which you knew you no longer belonged but instead of listening to your own knowingness, you stayed. Then, all of the sudden, the position ended, and you were free to go on the path your soul had been guiding you to.

It can be challenging at times, but I believe it's important to remember that very few things are so serious; to remember that all is well and we are always exactly where we are meant to be. If we can remember that everything we want is just waiting for us to be ready to call upon it, then life can be what it was meant to be all along: beautiful, easy, joyful and full of abundance.

Am I good enough? Even now, as I write this, I'm asking that question. That's okay, as long as I keep typing; as long as my arms are wide open to the opportunities and possibilities, as long as my feet keep moving, one step in front of the other. I'm focused on what I love, allowing that feeling to bubble up. That's the key to everything, all the time. It's about allowing the process to flow to you, finding joy which raises your vibration to match the level of that which you are seeking. It all falls together when you are so busy doing and enjoying that you no longer worry about what might not work. We all know that person who happily flows through life, and everything seems to fall right into line. You can be one of them.

It can be challenging to learn to trust the process, I'll be the first to admit that. And, as I personally attest, the process of writing is an excellent teacher. I wrote this book as part of a writing intensive, which was, well… *intense!* Each author in the intensive had a word goal based on what kind of book they were writing. My goal, for example, was forty thousand words, the length of a typical "self-help" book. At first, this was incredibly daunting. Sometimes it felt like running on a treadmill – you know, when it seems like you've been on it for fifteen minutes and then you look down and it's been three? I would write and write, only to find that I had barely made a dent in that word count. Then, two things shifted. First, I stopped focusing on the forty-thousand-word mark and instead focused on the smaller, daily milestones that would allow me to finish by the end of the intensive. This was about eight hundred-twenty words a day. I could do that!

More importantly, when I learned to stay in the present moment and enjoy the writing, the words really began to flow. When I felt discomfort, I breathed through it, and before I knew it I was enjoying every keystroke. I was enjoying the process of allowing the message to flow from my heart and onto the screen.

Developing my intuition, I would learn, also required patience and allowing. During a Reiki session, the practitioner told me that my spirit team wanted me to know my progress as an intuitive was basically "going as scheduled." In other words, I needed to exercise some patience, because it wasn't going to happen overnight (Why? Don't ask me). They compared me to a fine wine (actually, they just said wine; I added the fine part). The point was that just like the winemaker who must wait for the grapes to mature, I too had to allow the process, knowing that my gifts would come to fruition in perfect timing. Sometimes our abilities, be it intuition or anything else, needs time to ferment. And if we stop trying to rush it and lean into our faith, the harvest will be all the sweeter.

One afternoon, as my family drove to a friend's for dinner, the skies opened up into a lovely sun shower. Delighted, my daughter and I decided to look for the rainbow we were sure would be there. In a minute, we had the whole car looking for a rainbow. We looked on the way home too, but still, no rainbow. We were all a little disappointed. We knew there *should* be a rainbow out there. Later, the rainbow forgotten, we sat down to watch a movie.

All of a sudden, my son pointed excitedly toward the window and said, "Look, guys, a rainbow!" We looked out to see not one, but two beautiful multicolored arcs! It was breathtaking, as if the Universe had given us a double reward for our patience. Oftentimes, we assume what we desire will be delivered to us in a certain way and time because historically that is how it's gone or because we believe that's how things should unfold. We attach all sorts of restrictions, rules and timelines to it; then, when it doesn't arrive in the exact right time or form we expect, we give up and think it's just not coming, not going to happen. That rainbow was a beautiful reminder that if we allow the process to come in the timeframe that the Universe intends, we may just get a much better version of what we're asking for.

We came here to this earth to have fun, find joy and peace, and be challenged in the contrast when it shows up. We learn to move through the contrast, even when it feels complicated and overwhelming. As we do, it's important to give ourselves a break now and again. If we can do that, if we can allow ourselves just a moment of joy in the midst of the storm, we will be doing more to turn the tide than any amount of flailing or fighting. Just remember to look for the rainbow that might show up when you least expect it. It is not always easy to decipher things when you're in the thick of it, but that's the game. Watching from the sidelines may seem easier, but the victory is nowhere near as sweet.

There is a lot to be learned from competitive sports, especially those that involve a team. I played basketball in high school, and I remember one particular day watching from the bench. We all had been practicing our plays (how we were going to work together to get the ball through the net). We all knew where we were supposed to be and when we were supposed to be there. But for some reason, it wasn't working that way during the game. From my perspective on the bench, it was very easy for me to see what everyone was doing wrong. I knew immediately when one teammate was supposed to have crossed over already, and that another should have blocked the opposition under the net. Why couldn't they see that?

By the time I was called up, I was raring to go and show 'em how it's done… except that's not how it went. The coach started yelling at me to get across or block the opposition under the net, but I couldn't see what was going on, not from that same vantage point as I'd had from the bleachers. I had to adjust what I was doing based on what I could see in the now. And isn't the game of life the same? Sure, it would be easier to navigate if we could see everything that was happening or about to happen, but that's just not the way it works. Life is not about getting the play right every time or winning every game, it's simply about getting out there and playing the game, working on our skills and sharing them with our team. It's about finding ways to be just a little better than the day we were before.

Sometimes, just knowing you've hung in there despite all the penalties, setbacks and losses is the ultimate win. Most of us, at some point, have had to postpone a dream to take care of the business of daily life. We have kids to raise and/or bosses to please and bills to pay. Sometimes it seems the Universe is throwing everything at us all at once.

While writing this book, I was smack dab in the middle of chaos. We had sold our house, were building a new one, and were shuffling back and forth between our place at the lake and a relative's when we needed to be in town. Everything during that time was a curse and a blessing at once, but one constant in all of this was my inability to write. It seemed every time I tried, something at work or home would pull me away from it. Finally, I had to throw up the white flag and say, "Okay, life, you win. For right now, you win." And then the most amazing thing happened. As soon as I surrendered, it was as if the clouds of chaos parted. Before I knew it, I was sitting at the lake, watching my kids swim and relax, and I could focus on what had become my own heart's desire – to bring this message to you.

There will always be clouds of chaos moving their way into our lives, and they will always move out again. If we give ourselves a break, a little space to breathe and deal with (and learn from) whatever storm the clouds bring, we'll be stronger for it.

The Butterfly Effect

This theory, which is based on research conducted by MIT meteorologist Edward Lorenz during the 1970s, is about the interdependence of all things. Basically, something as simple as a tiny little butterfly flapping its wings in Brazil can set off a chain reaction that causes a tornado in Texas. Can you see the connection between this and our work here? Well, it is similar to throwing that pebble in the pond. The point is that if we can follow our hearts and fill ourselves up, our small actions are like the butterfly's and can make a big change by the time it gets to someone else. Our choices, whether positive or negative, change the world. Why not choose happiness and change the world for the better? Sometimes, the change is someone else's choice, and it simply affects us. At times, the changes create tornadoes in our own lives. We always have a choice and now the ball's in our court, so to speak. How do we continue the butterfly effect phenomenon? Do we transmute the energy or continue it? In other words, do we stop the negative flow of energy and choose to create positive change or continue with negativity?

I was pulling into the YMCA parking lot where my kids were at daycare. It's kind of a weird parking lot with parking for the main clients in one big space and then daycare pickup has its own little area. As you pull in, you take a quick left to go to the daycare parking instead of taking a right or going straight for the main parking. Anyway, I pulled in, there was someone behind me and someone about to try to leave from the main parking lot. At the same time, there were two people backing out of their parking spots in the little daycare area. Not knowing exactly what to do and trying to get out of the way, I pulled forward thinking that the main parking lot guy could weave around me and that the two backing out would be a bit faster. I wasn't really thinking, but I was trying to be polite. As I tried to get more out of the way, I was inching forward, closer to the car in front of me. She was waiting for the other car to back out of her spot and go. All of the sudden, I saw her looking into her side mirror, smiling (that smile that means you're an idiot and a jerk, and you shouldn't have done that) and shaking her head. I realized at that moment, the smile and the head shaking were for me!! She had assumed (at least I'm assuming) that I was being aggressive, and she was judging me for it. First, I was defensive and then my defensiveness turned to anger. I pulled into the spot, angry and spouting words at her, by myself in my car. And then I realized what I was doing. I had let the incident drag me down, and I didn't want to go there. I took a deep breath and did something completely different to get myself out of that funk. I think I returned a call to my husband. The point is first she made assumptions about me, not knowing anything about my motivations, my reasoning, who I am or where I had come from. And so did I. And why? Why make assumptions or if we're going to make assumptions, why can't we give each other the benefit of the doubt. Why can't we remember the other person might be distracted or angry for a very good reason, might be worried or stressed or confused. Why can't we assume the other person has the best intentions to do the right thing and then wait for them to prove us wrong? And why can't we stick together in this thing we're calling life. We are all down in the mucky muck, and wouldn't it be something if our dominant intent would be to lift each other up? I wanted to go find her and say, no I was trying to be nice, see? I was doing this, and I was doing that; actually, it was sort of the wrong thing to do, but I was trying to do the right thing. But why do we have to? Let's assume something different. But let's say I really was a jerk and aggressive and mean. How would I have gotten that way? Do we get like that from a life of love and compassion? Probably not. If you want to make a room brighter, you don't pull down the shades, you add more light. It we want people who are mean to be nicer/people who are hurting to be healed, we might be better off giving a little love and compassion. So, how do we do that when someone makes us angry or pushes our trigger buttons? It can be challenging. I certainly don't have all the answers, but it's helpful to start, I believe, by remembering why mean people are mean, and why aggressive people are aggressive. It might be because that's all they've ever known. And maybe you won't fix them or change them. But maybe you'll plant a tiny seed, one that you'll never see grow to a beautiful bouquet of kindness because maybe it will take a lifetime. But that doesn't mean we can't start trying to plant seeds. It's what mothers do. It's what the divine feminine leaders and way-showers do – the ones who know their power and use it to build others up versus tear them down. It is a life full of compassion, compassion for others but first for ourselves. And it starts with a patient quiet love that greets us like a whisper. It's deep down in our hearts past all the pain and fear, past the doubt and regret. It's deep in the garden, a seed of hope that will only grow when we are gentle with ourselves. Let's stay in this together and give each other a hand instead of pushing each other down, starting with ourselves.

Just like in the Y parking lot, sometimes we just need a little change of focus. Sometimes when we try to stare something down too long or when we try to fight our way through a problem or challenge, we get stuck, and all we need is a bit of a distraction.

One night I was putting my six-year-old son to bed. He was a little sick, at least he had a headache, and he was closing his eyes when his sister came in. I was a little annoyed because he looked like he was going to drift off to sleep quickly, and since he had a headache, I wanted him to get plenty of rest. Not to mention she was coming in to show him the recorder she had just gotten at school. Remember the recorder? They're not exactly the best medicine for a headache. But with her delicate, sing-songy, I'm happy and showing-my brother-something-nice voice, she said Ethan, do you want to see what I got at school today? A recorder, she quickly answered herself. And just like that his face slowly lit up and a smile came across his face. Cool, he said. You can play it, she said. He played a couple notes and giggled, cool! Then she left, and he happily went to sleep without one more peep about a headache. Sometimes when we are feeling down or can't quite shake whatever headache we are dealing with, the best medicine is to do something else altogether. Sometimes we just need a distraction to help us change our mood. Often, the most helpful thing you can do is to stop trying to figure something out or remember whatever it is you need to remember. Just the act of stopping gives our hearts just enough space to give us the answer. If something isn't working, walk away. When we give something a little space to breathe, it always seems to come to us – sometimes faster than we think.

We are trained our whole life to figure things out, to think and use our brain. Now it's time to begin to understand what our greatest teachers have long been saying…that the path to enlightenment is through the heart not the mind. It is through allowing not pushing. It's found in the love of what you are doing, no matter what it is, peace and acceptance in the now of the moment. When you feel a vibration of love, maybe overflowing into tears, you know you have reached the point where your heart is leading. That is how we will heal and create a world that is more beautiful than we could ever imagine. It is done through acceptance and a release of fear. It is done through love and a lack of judgment. It is done through freedom and gently demanding what makes you happy. Your happiness, my happiness will create a light that others will gravitate toward, and it will create space for them to begin to do the same.

Chapter 9

The Art of Saying No

What feelings does the word NO conjure up for you? If you're like many people, and depending on the context, it has a negative connotation, signifying disappointment, rejection or the act of letting someone down. You may not (yet) realize that those two sweet little letters can be one of the most important things you can say. In fact, for some people saying no is an art form, a way of gracefully stepping back and not taking on too much. Others, however, have such a difficult time saying it that they often find themselves overwhelmed, exhausted and resentful.

Saying no seems to be particularly difficult for women. It reminds me of a line from my favorite movie, *Pride and Prejudice:* "I've never met her, but she surely must be a fearsome thing to behold." In that scene Elizabeth Bennett is referring to a kind of super woman, a "Jaqueline of all Trades," able to do all sorts of things. It makes me wonder, though, if this woman was also able to say no! The truth is, probably not. We have been conditioned to please for so long, it has become second nature; we don't want to disappoint anyone. But we must learn to say it if we want to achieve balance in our lives.

How do we do this? The reality is, most of us are juggling jobs and kids and significant others. Everyone has needs, and in seeking to meet them all we tend to sacrifice ourselves. We become stretched too thin, and we can't get everything done. Then we end up with an empty tank and no way to replenish. We can't drive on an empty tank. We can't take care of others on an empty tank. When we try, we start to lose ourselves. Whatever fills us up or whatever brings us back to ourselves, it's time we do it. And it might just start by saying a no or two.

I know a woman who volunteered to be on the board of a budding non-profit, though in truth the role sounded more like that of a director. She said yes, despite the nudging of her heart that said maybe this wasn't right for her. Of course, as happens to so many of us, she didn't have the time to fulfill the obligation, and the director, fairly new at leading a non-profit, lacked the courage to ask her to step down. They had a discussion. The director skirted around the topic, and the two agreed to give it another try. A day or two later, the director called and asked the woman to step down from the board. What had started out as a well-intentioned act had become a source of self-judgement that she had not lived up to her commitment. Here's the thing: her only "failure" was in not listening to her heart, which was advising her to say no. We've been programmed to say yes to everything; now we have to reprogram ourselves to listen to that quiet whisper that says, "Well, dear, you can do this, or you can let this go with love and leave space open for the something more aligned to your soul's calling."

It's okay to say no to things that just don't feel right. You don't need an excuse. You don't need to apologize or feel guilty. You just need to be true to yourself. And when you say no, you are not only taking care of yourself; you are leaving that space open for someone who has been waiting for the very opportunity you have been offered. Win-win! It's not selfish to say no. It's not selfish to look after ourselves. It does take courage to say no. You are strong, and it is your strength that will inspire, lift and guide others.

> "You cannot get sick enough to help sick people get better. You cannot get poor enough to help poor people thrive. It is only in your thriving that you have anything to offer anyone. If you're wanting to be of an advantage to others, be as tapped in, tuned in, turned on as you can possibly be."
>
> **—Abraham Hicks**

When it's put that way it makes sense, right? The ability to say no is a reflection of our understanding of abundance, both with regard to the Universe and ourselves. Yet, when we try to apply this concept to our own life, it can be tempting to find reasons why it doesn't quite fit our situation. We were taught to believe in scarcity, that there's not enough to go around. What if the truth is just the opposite? What if there is enough for everyone, and the more we take care of ourselves, the more we can help become a light for others? We can go into it one day at a time, focusing on the wins and being gentle with ourselves when we don't quite hit the mark. Our health and abundance will not steal health and abundance from anyone else but rather provide an example of what is possible.

I still have to remind myself of this and counter the talk I hear from others and through my own inner dialogue. We built a two-story house. As we were considering it, part of me questioned whether we deserved to build something new when some don't have enough. I had to remind myself that building a house was a reflection of my abundance, not a reflection of anyone else's lack. And the same can be said for you. Now, is giving to others a good thing? Of course, it is, and we all do it in many ways, large and small. Sometimes we give through a donation to a local charity or through volunteering. Sometimes it's eye contact and a smile that reminds a homeless person of their dignity. Sometimes the only thing another person needs is to be seen. And yes, sometimes hearing no is what they need to hear in order to move forward and claim what is waiting for them.

When we maintain our own energy, it's easier to intuit what others need, and we have the strength to look after and care for them. When it comes to maintaining our strength, hummingbirds have a lot to teach us. They are small and delicate, the smallest bird, but despite their size they are very strong and fierce. They will aggressively protect their territory from other birds, including hawks. To stay strong, they must take in a lot of nourishment, up to half their body weight per day. To live like a hummingbird means to be delicate but strong. The two do not have to be mutually exclusive. To keep that strength, one must continually nourish oneself in whatever way is needed and that includes mind, body and spirit.

To put it another way, self-care is love for the only one who really matters in this world – you. You came here to grow your soul — not mine, not your significant other's and not even your children's. None of them need you. *You need you.* Can you stand in front of a mirror and say I love you? And, can you think of one way that you've shown yourself love? If not, get to it! (I'm saying that with love, of course.)

Chapter 10

Your Rules

We have all fallen prey to the many chains, bound together by beliefs and ideologies that are far past their time. The chains that hold us down are created from fears and old patriarchal patterns that are meant to restrict, not protect, hold back, not enable. And yet, with all that, it's easy to want to move to anger, but when we realize the chains that keep us in this prison-like existence are merely ideas and old stodgy beliefs, we can simply let them fall away, one by one. Plus, anger is simply another set of chains. Once we understand that those chains have made us stronger, made us more aware of the effects of our unchecked fear, we can give them love, allow them to dissolve, and walk away. We realize that we were never really trapped. We were using those experiences as a lesson and a launching point to be something more. They were our cocoon providing just the right challenge, reminding us of our strength. And when we emerge, we soar into our true destiny as the beautiful strong creature we were always meant to be.

The great poet Percy Bysshe Shelley wrote "The Masque of Anarchy," which encapsulates the irony and beauty in breaking free from the bondage we allow either knowingly or unknowingly.

He speaks of England, yet we speak of Earth, in all Her burgeoning glory:

> "What is Freedom? Ye can tell
> That which Slavery is too well,
> For its very name has grown
> To an echo of your own
> Let a vast assembly be,
> And with great solemnity
> Declare with measured words, that ye
> Are, as God has made ye, free.
> The old laws of England—they
> Whose reverend heads with age are grey,
> Children of a wiser day;
> And whose solemn voice must be
> Thine own echo—Liberty!
> Rise, like lions after slumber
> In unvanquishable number!
> Shake your chains to earth like dew
> Which in sleep had fallen on you:
> Ye are many—they are few!"

What are your chains? What is holding you back? Maybe it's a fear of seeing something you don't want to see or dealing with something you've safely tucked away. Or, as mentioned earlier, it can be a fear of allowing people to see us with all our perceived flaws and failures. Whatever the case, it has led to you to follow the rules of others, rather than your own.

Be "Good"; Follow the Rules

How many rules do you follow in a single day or an hour? Sometimes we call them "routines" and many times they are effective, no doubt. But often we get into a pattern of *Do this, then do that, then you can...* What if we instead started saying, "To heck with the rules?"

This is your game. You are at the controls. Make up the rules. Easy to say, not so easy to do, when we have been taught for so long to follow the rules laid down by others. Oftentimes we don't even question them or if they are even valuable; they have simply become a way of life. That's fine, remember, our soul will guide us to each truth as we are ready. Just start with the rules that are obvious rules and start to just ask why. Be curious. Maybe it's a speed limit in a school zone. Makes sense, go slowly so as to protect children who aren't always mature enough to follow the rules that keep them safe. We'll keep that one. It's the rules that don't feel right that we want to start to disrupt. The rules we follow just because it's what we've done or been told to do. Or the ones we've never even taken time to examine and maybe aren't actually a "rule" in the first place.

During week two of my eight-week writing intensive, I was supposed to be working on the book outline. Except, I had already written some of the content. I could use that content to help fill in the outline, right? Our instructor had never said we could do that. After hemming and hawing, I finally said, "This is ridiculous. I can look at the content! Why am I so stuck on what the rules are? And they weren't even rules – it was just what she said to do. She never said it was a rule. I interpreted it as a rule. I had boxed myself in without even realizing it and without needing to.

How do inventors and entrepreneurs make great advances and create the next cool gadget or disruptive technology? They break every rule they can. They come up with big ideas and fail fast. They learn to pivot and keep breaking the rules until a broken rule becomes the latest solution, until it becomes the rule.

Once we've started to observe all the rules, boxes really, around us, what's next? How do we learn to break free, and what rules do we break? What are the rules for breaking the rules? As is so often the case, it starts with the heart. We trust our heart and do what feels right. Maybe we can trust that if we do more of what nourishes our soul, it will give others permission to do the same.

When my son was six, he was very energetic. Wow. It was hard to get him to focus, so hard in fact that folks were telling me that he should be on medicine. Based on the rules of modern society, to be in school, to be successful, you need to be calm, sit in your seat, blah, blah. I knew before I saw any doctor that some of those rules were going to have to change. I knew in my heart I was going to need to break those rules. I needed to follow my own heart, and my son's, to determine what we would do to support his success. And if he were to go on medicine, it would be our choice, not because a doctor said so. The point is that the rules may provide useful guidelines in a given situation, but they are never a substitute for your own inner knowing about the right path for you.

Another set of rules women often come up against are those governing how they should balance being a mother with their career. What if your greatest wish is to stay at home for a year with your kiddos? Why can't you do that? It may be because of those people buzzing in your ear that you'll no longer be marketable. Once you're out of the workforce, that's it, you're damaged goods. And all of the sudden, that becomes your truth. Obeying that rule, we trudge to work, day after day, afraid to claim the freedom we desire. Who says we can't take a year off and then get back into the work game? Or maybe you have a whole different option. Maybe there is a way for you to work and be at home. If we are making our own rules, let's really get creative. Once we start imagining life exactly the way we want and then expect it to be, it's amazing how many things will suddenly fall into place to make our vision a reality. It may not happen all at once, but if we can hold the vision and expect it to happen, it will eventually manifest in our world. It can really be that easy. It's as easy as we let it be. Why can't we have it all, whatever our "all" is? Why can't we create our perfect life? Let's break some rules.

Why Sometimes It's Okay to Step Back Instead of Leaning In...

Back when I was a VP of marketing, my boss and the president of the organization encouraged me and two colleagues to start working with an agency that could help us identify and eliminate any gaps hindering our ability to lead the organization. The plan was to work with them for a year or more, but a few months into the process my boss decided to retire. He also encouraged me to apply for his position. Up to that point, I wouldn't have considered myself even remotely qualified, but now I was seriously considering it. If he saw a leader in me, maybe I was one! That said, I wasn't wearing rose-colored glasses; I wasn't expecting to get the position. My boss explained that this would give me experience with the hiring process and would cause people to consider me a serious candidate the next time around.

I wanted to want it. I thought of all the women who don't have the opportunity, the confidence or whatever. I knew I could do the role. I had the ideas and the energy, and I believed I could rise to the occasion. *I wanted to want it...but I didn't.* When I thought of all the roads I could travel, this one just didn't fill me with excitement like some others. It wasn't really something I wanted to fight for. Did I need to? I really did wrestle with that question. I thought of the book *Lean In* and how more women need to take chances, push themselves, trust that they are capable. And I have all that. But right at that moment, with little kids and other dreams, I just didn't want to. That job, that ladder of success just felt like a box created from a masculine 3D world. It's not bad; I just knew there was something different for me. I was ready to allow "something different" to manifest so I could create a different story. I wanted to rise into my feminine power and not just change the world but remind it how to heal itself. I didn't want to be part of a masculine-created, top-down hierarchy. I didn't even know what my "something different" would look like, and I wanted to step back, or maybe more accurately, step onto my true path. And I did.

Let's give ourselves a moment to step back when we need to. Let's trust the Universe to open the path to what is for our best and highest good. Let's breathe and allow our true gifts to emerge again. And give ourselves a break. We don't have to be here to fight all the time. We can allow, because I believe when we allow, our hearts pull to us what we most desire. And I'm not settling. I'm growing into something even more aligned with me and my path. Are you?

Moving through my life, I have begun to ask so many questions and some of my questions have centered around my faith. I was raised in the ELCA Lutheran church, which is fairly easygoing, as Lutherans don't really like to be told what to do. It was comfortable; not too many rules, just allow Jesus to do most of the heavy lifting. But at some point, some of the words and ideas behind the religion started to conflict with what felt right in my heart. Suddenly I felt at odds with my religion, the one thing that was keeping me "safe" or, more accurately, boxed me in with the illusion of safety.

I can best describe this shift in this way: it began to feel like the pastors (our shepherds) were using an old, old map to get us (their sheep) from our pasture to the water. Almost all the sheep were following, no questions asked, not even looking up. I sat there watching them as they followed blindly to a murky water, then began drinking just as blindly. I had created my own perfect, pristine water, yet when I looked down at it I realized I was afraid to drink. Why isn't anyone else making their own water? Is there something wrong with my water? Is it too good to be true, a trick? Should I be ashamed of this water? Is it bad?

I could see even some of the shepherds started to look confused, their brow wrinkled as they studied the old map. They sensed it too, it seemed. I knew that I would need to make a choice because I couldn't do both, but I'd become unsure. So for the time I followed the herd, all the while knowing there was another way. Knowing soon I would step bravely onto a new path, one I was meant to follow all along. For some shepherds, there is no doubt. They are sure of the map; they are sure of the path and are most comfortable leading their flock to the murky waters. And that path is fine, the trail is worn and easy to see, and there is truth there too. The water is fine too and provides all they need. And can both paths be true and good? Can our truth be a kaleidoscope of varying colors and angles that together create a beauty that couldn't be seen any other way? Is it time to go beyond one truth, one color, one angle and allow more?

Take this book for example. There are a lot of great things in it that have worked for me. It contains things I do to remind myself that I am a spirit in human form, things to get me back to my center. And some of them might work great for you too. But some of them might feel off or not work for you at all. That's okay. If you only take one thing from this book, from me, let it be the reminder that you already have all you need. And your team will guide you to yourself. You'll find it in the synchronicities, in the happenstance things that pull you to a book or a recording. You might learn about a technique that really allows you to embrace the love you are or reminds you to be present in the moment. You might meet a mentor who helps you heal a wound. You make the rules for your life. No one can live it for you, nor would you want them to. You have the freedom and the responsibility to live this life to your fullest, to follow your own path and to be guided by the gentle calling of your heart. It's time to drop into our own knowing; our hearts can lead us to our own set of rules or lead us to a life with, dare I say, no rules at all.

Chapter 11

Your Life Brought You Here

Look at the lessons in your life, see the path as it unfolds.

One morning my coworker and I left the office and headed for one of our go-to coffee shops, only to find that it was closed for the day. We began walking downtown toward a different coffee shop, and about halfway there we remembered yet another coffee shop that we really liked. We changed course and went to this quaint little coffee shop in the basement of a building just a block or two away. We got our coffee, and as we were leaving, my coworker picked up a flyer and showed it to me. It was for a class that I ended up taking and really loved. A few simple changes of our course had led me to a flyer I would have never found for a class I would have never taken had I not made those changes. I had just benefited from a beautiful thing called synchronicity.

As we start to trust and follow the breadcrumbs our angels or spirit team lays out for us, we will begin to experience all sorts of synchronicities. Merriam-Webster defines synchronicity as "the coincidental occurrence of events and especially psychic events (such as similar thoughts in widely separated persons or a mental image of an unexpected event before it happens) that seem related but are not explained by conventional mechanisms of causality." When we begin to focus on what we want (without getting caught up in the details) and how we want to feel, synchronicities will happen with more and more frequency. The Universe wants to guide us to an abundance of joy. Synchronicity will lead us piece by piece, little by little on a winding road toward our goal. And often, our angel guides will lead us to so much more than we could dream up ourselves...if we are open. If we trust.

We are all receiving guidance from Spirit, all the time. Sometimes a synchronicity will bring me a job and then as I go through the process, I begin to doubt my value and my ability to do it. For some reason I start to doubt that Spirit will continue to help me, as if the flow of abundance will stop right after the opportunity. For some reason I believe that I'll get the job and then won't be able to come up with the ideas or the inspiration to succeed. Why is it that I believe that it only goes part way? Why do I believe that God or Spirit will only guide me to enough inspiration to get the freelance marketing gig or whatever opportunity presents itself? Why do I believe that once the job is in hand, the free flow of inspiration will stop? The answer is that it wouldn't unless I stopped it. If I continue to be open, the Universe will provide me all the opportunities and abundance I can handle. My work is simply to get out of my own way. My work is to heal the wound(s) that prevents me from trusting Source.

It is our natural state to remember that we are powerful and intuitive, and every choice is the right choice, every experience the exact right experience for our soul's growth. Trust your feelings, follow them. This process is a bit like boiling a pot of water. Like the water, you might not notice the changes happening inside you, but you are warming up. When you heat water to boil, it gets warm first and to your eye it looks the same until it's boiling. Until then you just trust that it will boil when the conditions are right. When you are ready, you will start to see changes. But before that, when you begin to invite the Universe in to help you, you will start to see those "coincidences" and if you are willing to follow them, they will continue to guide you to yourself. Your true self. And little by little you will unfold, you will peel off layer by layer all the stuff that no longer serves you. You will uncover the authentic you. You will remember the reason you came here. You will shine in your truth and in the full power of your light. And the world will be better for it. In fact, it already is. Stand in love, be at peace. And know that you are ever-unfolding, glorious in your true form. You are pure love, nothing less. You deserve all you can imagine and more. And so it is.

Simple changes one at a time lead to big results.

There are times when we want to make a change or accomplish a goal, but the thing we desire seems so far from our grasp. The grandness of it is paralyzing. Sometimes it's okay to simply say to the Universe, "I am ready, and I'm going to take one step, however small. After that I will allow the Universe to guide me slowly the rest of the way." Truly, we've already been doing it all our lives, now it's time to do it with intention.

So, what does that look like?

Let's say we really want to run marathons, but we've spent most of our life on the couch. We wouldn't sign up for the Boston Marathon, which needs a qualifying run, not to mention a lot of training. Or, take a much smaller example: you commit to drinking the eight to ten glasses of water a day, for better health. Currently, you drink mostly soda. You say, "Okay, Universe, this is me taking my desire and putting it into action to better myself." You say, "Here I am, Universe." Then you focus on that one thing to better yourself, trusting that the Universe will help. It's easy and fun, and you start to notice how much better you feel. You make a plan: drink two glasses when you wake up, two more before lunch, two in the afternoon and two around dinner. Even if you miss one or two, you've reached your goal.

Starting with water might seem very small, but the point is to make a commitment to yourself and the Universe that you're in this. And adding water to your diet heals your body. Once you start healing, you crave more of it. More ways to heal start flowing to you, for example, enjoyable ways to move your body. The Universe will know the changes you're making and the shift in your intent, and it will respond in kind. It has to. As energetic creatures, we are shifting our own energy around with every thought and action. Those shifts cause other things to shift and respond. One step, one change ripples out.

The marathon is a larger goal, but it's the same principle. Once you start taking the steps (i.e. getting off the couch) you might be surprised how many things start to fall into place, taking you along your path to what you truly desire. You find a group that walks together. Maybe there's someone in the group you really connect with, and you find out that person also wants to run a marathon, and you start training together. And it's fun. Just take one step, make one change (and open yourself up to the Universe) and that might make all the difference in the world. Before you know it, you're crossing that finish line. It's about trusting and allowing the process to unfold. And taking one little step, the one that feels right. And then taking another step when the Universe connects you to it. It's about getting back on track when you get off track. And it's about not giving up. Remember how much you are worth, and you'll never give up.

Remember too, that those steps you take unintentionally can also effect significant change in your life (i.e. things you don't want). Therefore, it's important to be conscious of all the choices we make and the beliefs we hold.

Everything Happens for a Reason

It's so easy to worry or to get distracted by all sorts of little things that fall into our path, and it's important to trust and to take our journey one step at a time. And if I dare say, have fun once in a while or (gasp!) all the time.

A while back, while growing a business, I came up with an idea for a T-shirt that I thought would be empowering for young girls. Once we created the t-shirt design, the idea spread to other ideas. At the same time a friend and I (we were both in marketing and public relations) began getting freelance inquiries. It was exciting, and I wanted to talk about it with others, but I noticed that when I mentioned our potential freelance gig to other people, they would start talking about their own freelance business (or those of someone they knew), and they would begin rattling off all the complications that could arise. And there were a lot. It was kind of awful. Yet I just kept moving forward with one idea, one little step. I trusted my heart, and I worked on what felt right. I focused as much of my attention as I could on the things that filled me up and got me excited. I worked on and dreamed about the things that really made me happy.

Back to the t-shirt. While on a retreat I met a designer who I immediately trusted. I listened to my heart and gave her the bid. She did the work, and it was beautiful. The design was low-cost, and it all worked out great. Had I listened to those negative messages from others (the potential pitfalls of going into business with someone else or the pain of freelancing, the taxes, et cetera), I would have been sunk. Of course, listening to advice that directs you to the easiest path is always welcome, but there's a big difference between the two. You can feel it. Planning is one thing. Worrying and stopping because of those worries is a whole different thing altogether. We can achieve anything we desire, if only we can close out some of the negativity and learn to trust our heart, take it one step at a time and allow the Universe to guide us to each step.

One day I was driving behind a truck with the words, "Explore life one sip at a time" painted on it. Granted, it was for some kind of alcohol, but it was a great message, nonetheless. It's about exploring the adventure that is life, while taking it one step at a time and really enjoying every bit of it. The beautiful thing is that we don't have to know everything. We don't want to down the whole drink at once. It would be too much. We are given just what we can handle. While you can enjoy the thought of the bigger glass or the bigger picture, the power is in that moment, in each sip. The small moments that all make up the big ones, and when we falter or forget, the reminders are everywhere, even on the back of an alcohol truck on your way to work.

Climbing a Mountain...

When we climb a mountain, we don't pause to wonder why we can't see the entire landscape, we just keep climbing because we know there's more to go. We understand that eventually we'll get to the top and will be able to see the beauty that lies below us. And yet, as we move through our own personal journeys climbing our metaphoric mountains, we tend to wonder why we aren't already there, why we can't see the landscape. Then, when we do reach the top of a mountain, we don't stop to look around and enjoy the view because we've already started on the next mountain. Can you take a moment to enjoy the landscape of your life? Can you stop and appreciate how far you've come, what you've weathered and what you've accomplished?

Sometimes it's best to do the work and just put one foot in front of the other with faith. As we move, we suddenly realize that we are starting to see around the corner, and it was as good as we thought and oftentimes even better. And that's life, full of corners that demand our faith - faith in ourselves, faith in life and faith in the path. We uncover what we need one rock at a time.

Go ahead and breathe life into your dreams with your joy, your love, your willingness to get quiet and just be.

Chapter 12

Life Reflects What You Need

Your whole life is one big mirror, and it's there for your healing. Have you ever said, "Why is this happening to me?" Or, "Why does this ALWAYS happen to me?" How about shifting those words to, "Why is this happening for me?" Or, "What is this experience here to teach me?"

If we can look at the things that ruffle our energy, that make us angry or afraid, we'll see them as the doors to our liberation, an invitation to heal. If we create some space for awareness and to feel it, whatever we struggle with internally will reveal our blocks. Our emotions are just like a set of auto gauges, indicating what needs attention. Anger and jealousy are covering up pain and a need for love and healing. Listen and observe yourself and you can heal the things holding you back. For example, when I was younger, I was talking to a couple of friends who were a little older than me. While I can't remember the exact conversation, I didn't understand something that they were saying. They laughed at me and called me an airhead, and I was devastated. I went home and told my dad what had happened. My dad listened intently to my story, and when I was done, he asked if I'd be upset if they'd said I was fat. I laughed, and I said well no because I wasn't fat. That sounded ridiculous to me. My dad smiled and asked, "So why did it bother you that they called you an airhead?" He went on to explain that maybe it bothered me because on some level I feared it was true. It bothered me because on some level I believed them. I doubted myself and wondered if I was good enough in that way and so it revealed my doubt and insecurities. His wise words shined a light on a wound and gave me an opportunity to feel and release it. We all have those opportunities all the time... a choice to heal our wounds or bury them.

On Facebook I reconnected with an old high school acquaintance. Through his posts, he had expressed a few rough times — depression, breakups et cetera. One day, he posted that he was offended by people who said that for others to love you, you first must love yourself. Now from one perspective, he is right. We are all worthy of love, whether we love ourselves or not. That said, the truth is that the world reflects our beliefs. If we don't believe we are worthy of love, the Universe will deliver that (our feeling of unworthiness) to us on a silver platter. We will see reflections of the love we lack for ourselves. But how do you start to feel worthy and remember how to love yourself? How do you heal?

Start small. Go ahead and find something simple to appreciate. Maybe it's the beautiful sunset or a new pillow, so comfortable, so perfect that it amazes you, and you smile just thinking about it. Or maybe it's just the idea that a pillow means rest. You can focus on the happiness and the warm fuzzy feeling that comes when you snuggle your head into your pillow and close your eyes. The world washes away as you sink into the pillow's perfect softness, sleep greeting you like a friend. Allow the smile to come across your face when you think of it. Feel the calmness that comes when you lay your head down. Now think about those things in your life that represent that kind of experience — your own pillow experience, if you will. Let yourself get lost in the feeling of it for just a moment. The longer you can settle into that feeling, the better off you'll be. It strengthens your ability to attract all the good things you would like in your life. Let the good feelings flow in and remember that they are always there waiting for you to tap into them. That is how we begin to uncover our garden, our dreams. We do it just a little at a time, allowing ourselves to be happy and to appreciate first little things until they grow into bigger things. As the appreciation takes us closer to our garden, we also begin to attract others who feel the same as us, and we begin to tap into the energy and connect to the resources to make even bigger steps.

For many of us, it's difficult (and at times impossible) to see the beauty within ourselves. I had a friend who was so beautiful, but I knew she couldn't see it. In fact, she was quite hard on herself. Her self-hate stemmed from her relationship with her mother, and she had neither the tools nor had the capacity to dig down and work through her trauma. It appeared that she was not even aware of it. Knowing that, I realized that giving her books or telling her how to move past her negative self-tendencies wasn't going to help her. What might help, though, was to be within a circle of healing energy, a nurturing circle of love and wisdom, where others could serve as the light so she could begin to find the beauty that is illuminated within her.

If you continue to interact with people who trigger the same emotion within you, you can be sure the Universe is providing a mirror for you. So, if you come across person after person who makes you angry or irritated, and they all tend to do the same thing, you might want to take a serious look at the gift the Universe is sending you. It's an invitation from your higher self for your own healing and growth. You're welcome.

There was a woman I worked with who could drive me up a wall faster than anyone or anything else I could think of. She was a major trigger for me. In all honesty, she could trigger pretty much everyone in our office. In her defense, she was a very kind person, and probably unaware that she triggered folks as she did. She didn't need to because the healing was for the ones she triggered.

I remember asking a mentor what to do, and how I could deal with whatever trigger she was triggerin' so she could get the heck out of my life. Of course, working through the trigger doesn't necessarily mean the person leaves. They might, but they can also just stop being a trigger. You respond differently to their energy, and you begin to deal with (what feels like) a different person altogether.

Now, back to my trigger-tripping coworker. It would happen so suddenly that it would catch me off guard. We could be talking about some issue, something on the news, or I could be innocently sharing something I'd done or changed. All of the sudden she would begin talking about her belief about the way life was or should be based on her interpretation of life, thanks to her faith. Or she would ask me about my children, then immediately launch into a long-winded, one-sided conversation about her own child. Basically, inquiring about me was just an opening to talk about her life. Then there was the trigger of all triggers – her "ability" to argue her point. And she seemed to have a point about everything. She would go on and on, and if I tried to get a word in edgewise, she would talk a little faster, then a little louder and would ignore any attempted interjections. After she exhausted her argument, I would have a chance to say my piece, but I had to be fast. At that point, she would quickly walk away, leaving me fuming. I would then find myself first complaining to my other coworker, all the while wondering why I was so darn irritated. So I journaled it out a bit, and to be honest it didn't take long because I'd been working through this for a while; I just hadn't taken the time to get quiet and allow the answer to come up from my heart instead of my head for a change. My head had all sorts of explanations that frankly weren't getting me anywhere. That's because my head wanted to make it about her when really it was about me. When I started asking what bothered me about it, my heart started to communicate the lesson. The woman triggered me because she made me feel not listened to. She made me feel like I wasn't worthy of being heard and understood. I felt like I wasn't important enough to be listened to, not important enough to have a say, to get a turn.

I am worthy, and I want to feel worthy. I deserve to feel important enough to have a turn. My thoughts are worthy, and I have good things to say. I want to teach, and I can't teach love if no one is listening. Now when I write those things down, I feel more open. It feels like I'm releasing something real. It brings real emotion, emotion I've been storing, that's been weighing me down. It's a process so I've been dealing with this a few different times, a few different ways.

Here's another example. An office where I worked had an arrangement where one person would work Friday afternoons so the others could have it off. We all took turns, but one particular Friday hadn't been picked up. A coworker felt like she got stuck holding the bag, and she wasn't happy about it. When she came into my office to vent, I was a little surprised. I remember thinking, *Then just say I can't do it" or don't say anything at all.* The more I thought about it, the more irritated I became; after all, it wasn't my fault. I had worked my fair share of Fridays. This wasn't my energy to carry. To release the trigger, I pretended she and I were both in the office, and I let her have it. I yelled at her for not speaking her truth, for not saying what she wanted and for taking it out on me. Then (and this was powerful for me), I turned her image into my own. Because I was really yelling at myself. Because the world is simply a reflection for our own growth and healing. Once I changed her image to mine, it was quite amazing. I felt the emotions, and I released them.

I continue to work with my triggers, trusting my feelings, my higher self to guide me. It's like peeling the layers off an onion; each time you work through a trigger, allowing it in, feeling it, letting it speak to you and releasing it, you peel another layer. Or, think of it as pulling another weed to get to the beauty of your garden. Triggers are sneaky that way, they are always wanting to make sure we're healed. Those people who becomes triggers in our lives are in service to our soul, allowing us to see and heal something inside. When we realize that, it's easier to be grateful.

How would we learn compassion if everything in our life were "perfect"? When we force ourselves, through outside circumstances, to learn forgiveness, we are giving ourselves such a gift. The life path we carve for ourselves is for our soul's growth, and we grow from lessons, both easy and challenging. We learn kindness from experiencing the opposite. We learn to be soft because we see where being hard gets us. And even though we aren't aware of the path we set before ourselves in the now of this soul journey, we can see the parallel in how we learn in this life. Think about the ways you have chosen to challenge yourself. Maybe it was in school when you decided to take a more difficult class. You knew at some point it was going to get challenging, but you did it anyway. And in the middle, when you were at the most difficult point, you steeled yourself for the task and kept going until you made it to the light at the end of the tunnel. And you were wiser, braver and a bigger version of you in the end. That is why we are here. If we allow the experiences "good" or "bad," to flow to us and just give ourselves some credit, we will come out the other side with the gift of our experiences to teach us who we really are. We deserve to see what we are capable of, and that's why we came to this beautiful planet we call Earth.

As we amp up our power by being present in the now, we allow the beauty of contrast to guide us back to our soul. I grew up on a farm in eastern North Dakota. On the farm there was a piece of equipment called a manure spreader. If you are not familiar with farming it may surprise you, but it's exactly as it sounds. It spreads poop from the farm animals, and it goes all over your field. It's a real thing. You can look it up. Of course, as you are probably aware or can guess, the manure fertilizes the field and helps grow better crops. My dad always called that disgusting smell "the smell of money." So, I guess the lesson here is to let the poop of your life be the fertilizer for your soul. It's okay to laugh once in a while.

What a wonderful world. Contrast is great fertilizer for our growth. Not only does it allow us to better sift through what we want and don't want, it allows us to grow more fully into who we are meant to be, more of ourselves. And isn't that what we're here for? I'd say it is.

According to Abraham Hicks (and other spiritual leaders), you can enjoy the contrast because it helps you make choices. Sure, it's easy to be in a blissful state at home when the conditions are optimal. True mastery is being able to maintain a state of peace no matter where you're at and no matter what is happening. Can you maintain your calm in the eye of the storm? You meet your life from a place of gratitude, peace and love.

Consider the person who drives you crazy the most — who are they, and why do they bother you so much? What if we could see deep into their soul and know just what drives them to those annoying tendencies, those off-the-wall beliefs or those mean comments, whatever it is? What if we could see the child belittled by his father, or the girl who spent her youth listening to her mother tell her she was fat? What if we could see the continual torment that child went through and the rough time they had at school or in college or how they cried themselves to sleep night after night? What if we could truly understand what makes them tick so that we could love who they are, even while we disagree with what they do? What if we could separate the person from the action? That doesn't mean you stay with a cruel person or say, "Well, they were abused so it's okay." It just means maybe we can allow ourselves to view the person as a person of light who simply acted in a way that doesn't align with who we (or they) are at a soul level. We all make choices, and sometimes we look back only to wish we'd made a different one. Yet at the same time we like to compare and say, "Well my 'bad' choices weren't nearly as bad as his or hers." But what if the scale is completely arbitrary? What if it's all a lie? What if we are here to experience? What if when the curtain closes on this life, we get up, walk away from the stage and laugh at the crazy things we experienced? What if we walk away at peace no matter "how bad" the things were that happened to us?

We tend to believe that only the good things are good. Every one of our experiences brings us growth if we allow it, and the things we believe are negative or unwanted experiences can become the richest soil for our soul's expansion once we heal it. Our most beautiful opportunities happen from the darkest places. It might be a loss or a rejection. It might be a seeming failure.

Take the lotus flower. It's a beautiful delicate flower, and as it grows, it rises above the mud. The lotus flower is perfectly and beautifully symbolic as it grows up out of muddy places. Sometimes it's best if we just settle into the mud and allow it to nourish us in a way that nothing else could. Once we have received all the nourishment we need, we begin to grow into the beautiful flower we were always meant to become. Fall gracefully into the darkness because only through the mud shall we rise.

Chapter 13

Owning Our Truth

When I was in college, my boyfriend cheated on me. A lot. To say I was devastated when I found out would be a gross understatement, not only because of his betrayal, or because I felt like I was the last person (maybe on the whole campus) to know, but because I no longer knew who I was. I didn't know how to define myself after that experience. How awful, how unworthy must I be for him to cheat on me like that! I saw his cheating as a reflection of myself, rather than a result of his own lousy choices.

This experience forced me to face the fact that I had put my self-worth in someone else's hands. This was a jarring realization indeed, but a blessing as well. I learned that I alone was responsible for how I felt about myself. This experience also taught me to trust my intuition. I always knew deep down what he was doing, but I doubted the feeling. I never knew I could rely on this inner knowing.

Over time I eased my way into healing. Slowly, I peeled back each layer of the experience, each one revealing a new, raw wound. Some of our wounds seem big and are easy to spot. Others are a little (or a lot) more subtle and go way back to our little selves, who had been bruised and battered by this harsh 3D energy.

Many of these wounds are inflicted by others, often without their knowledge and intention. I remember one Saturday, long ago, when I decided to not wear makeup. When I went into the kitchen, I found my dad sitting there with his farmhand. Dad asked if I was sick, then the kid looked at me with concern and reiterated the question. I said, nope I felt fine, but all of a sudden I didn't feel fine. I felt ugly. I went back into my bedroom and put makeup on. And ever since, I can't leave the house without eyeliner and mascara. A part of me died a little that day, stepped back into the shadows, head down, covered in a cloak of sadness, in a new belief in my unworthiness, my lack. How do I bring her back? How do I put life back into her cheeks, sing love into her soul? How do I love her back into being? What is beauty? Do I need it anyway? Do I cry? Do I get angry? How do I heal that part of me that won't come out?

You may be inclined to be angry with my father and his farmhand, but, really, they were just mirroring my own fears back to me. Playing out a game for me to experience my lack so I could find my worth. It just took me – is taking me – some time to recognize it as such. It has taken me time to shed the cloak and raise my sword to cut back all that I am not and to demand I see the truth of who I am. Because in truth, this is my game, only me and the kaleidoscope of reflections I have placed in my path. Will I ever walk out of the house without makeup on? I don't know, and that's okay. For now, I'll practice looking into the mirror and seeing the love that I am, made up or not.

Can we accept who we are right at this moment? Can we look down at our untoned stomachs, our hair that is starting to turn grey, our laugh lines or our face that's too full or has too many freckles, and just say, "Wow, I'm amazing. I can do this and that." Can we appreciate our bodies for all that they do for us? Can we say more often things like, "I enjoy life, and I am stunning for all of my attributes"? Can we realize that for all the ways in which we think we are less than, someone else might look at with envy? That if by loving ourselves completely, without restriction, we can become the thing we have always wanted to be? Whatever we love grows and flourishes. What if by talking to ourselves with love, we can change the energetic structure of our bodies?

There is evidence of this in Dr. Masaru Emoto's famous experiments with water. Emoto took several water samples, exposed them to various types of sounds, then studied them under a high-powered microscope. The water samples that had been exposed to positive words or classical music looked like perfect, unique snowflake designs. Those that were exposed to negative words or harsh, heavy metal music, had distorted, "unpleasant" shapes. If you consider that experiment and remember that our bodies are made up of fifty to seventy percent water, it becomes clear how important what we hear, including what we tell ourselves, is to our wellbeing. Also keep in mind that babies have the highest percentage of water, around seventy-five percent, then drop to sixty to seventy percent range when they turn one. Imagine what all those negative sounds would do to them. All the more reason to flood their homes with Beethoven and I love yous!

We have much to learn from those water experiments. Each one of your cells works hard every day to be its best little cell self, waiting for you to notice it. When we really think about all the things our bodies do, often without our conscious input, it's pretty amazing. Yet all too often we are incredibly critical of and hard on our bodies. Imagine what would happen to our bodies if we instead looked at them with gratitude, if we nourished them and gave them the same encouragement we would give a friend: eat healthier, exercise more (or perhaps less - my knees don't thank me for some of those crazy exercises). We don't try to build others up by tearing them down, so why should we do it to ourselves? Let's try something new.

Stoking the Fire of a New Idea

When your idea is new and young, it's important to be careful with it, like delicate embers in a fire. Like a fire, if you push too hard, it's too much and the fire goes out. Conversely, if you do nothing, the fire dies for lack of tending. The beginning can be a delicate balance; thankfully, your heart knows just what to do.

I believe that as we move into any endeavor but especially a new one, it's important to only focus on the success of it. It's important to focus only on that which gives you confidence in your ability to do the things you've set out to do. Tell only those who will honor your idea and encourage you. If there is something or someone who makes you doubt yourself or that it can happen, stop. Just take a break from that person or that thing that causes doubt.

When I was writing this book, I was part of a Facebook writing group. The group was great. They were very supportive of each other and when someone published his/her book or made it to a bestseller list, everyone cheered them on. I bought their books and did what I could to share; I would also read excerpts or descriptions of their work. And I would panic. Either the topic was too close to mine, or I was afraid I would accidentally plagiarize their content. It got to the point that while I was writing my first draft, I had to take a limited role within the FB group. I just couldn't read the works of other authors because it would make me doubt myself. Then once I let the doubt build up inside me, I would find myself super busy with all these other "very important" tasks (see the earlier section about cleaning out the closets), none of which got me closer to finishing my book. In other words, my ego took over and kept me busy, kept me safe from failure, safe from ridicule. It also kept me from reaching my goal, it kept me from stretching past my current state. It kept me from stepping past fear and into a bigger me.

We live in a society that rewards and stresses the process of thinking through everything, using our heads versus our hearts and our intuition. But sometimes heads overthink and get us into trouble. We worry about this or that and worry ourselves out of doing the "thing." When we drop into our hearts, we can find a wisdom that our heads just can't quite grasp. Think of those times when you relied on your heart – were you ever disappointed? History is full of examples of people who ignored their heads and followed their heart, their passion, with incredible success. Whether it's an invention or business, a cause or a belief, our heart can feel into the subtle realms, allowing us to tap into the universal mind where true creativity is found.

And what about the Dream Crushers? You know who I'm talking about. The people in your life who tell you "how it is." They "bring you back to reality." When you tell them your idea, or you tell them what you're going to do, they respond with why your idea won't work or what's not going to go well. I'll give you an example. At one point when I was writing this, I was talking to a friend about the book and how I wanted to be a public speaker and go out and promote my book that way. The first thing this well-intentioned friend said was something like, "Boy, do you realize all the traveling you'll have to do? You'll be gone every week for speaking engagements." On and on he went, making sure I understood all the negative aspects of my grand idea. And though I just nodded and smiled and said, "Yeah that could be," I have to admit it stuck with me a little bit. Thankfully, I was in a good place overall and understood my decision and what I intended to manifest so I could work through it and put it aside. Without this awareness, however, it can be easy to get derailed, either by those who are trying to keep us safe or, to be honest, may have less altruistic motives. That's why it's important to guard our hearts and our dreams, especially in the early stages.

How can we manage situations when others, including those closest to us, drop little bits of negativity onto our idea? First, it's important to discern whether or not they are well-intentioned. If so, we must honor what they are trying to do and say thank you for trying to protect us. Regardless of their motives, we can send them love and then just take their negative comment or energy, put it on a cloud and let it float up. Then say, "Thank you, Universe, for the contrast because I have other ideas and this will not work in my reality. I choose for this to be easy and fun and light, and I will continue with my dream, trusting, and letting it unfold. And so it is." How does that feel? Lovely? Powerful?

We are divine creators and words are ours to use as we wish. By themselves they are just that, words. But with energy and feeling behind them, they are magic. They can be extremely powerful if we give them that power. If we let them go, if we decide we don't agree, then they hold no power over us. Words plus feeling creates.

Chapter 14

Create Your Own Circle of Wisdom

I remember when I was younger, I would spend all day with my friends and then go home and talk to my best friend for hours on the phone. We could spend all night talking. What did we even talk about for that long after spending all day together? Who knows, but whatever it was, it was important and fun. Most of us have these kinds of childhood stories; then, somewhere along the line, we lost that connection. We got the idea that we had to go it alone.

As we grow into adulthood, we tend to compartmentalize our lives and the people in it. We do this, or we don't do that. We do certain things with certain friends and other things with others; some we speak to on the phone but rarely see. For example, if we have kids and a friend doesn't, we assume we no longer have much in common with them. Maybe we can decide to get out of our rut and carve out some more time to spend together. I once spent three days scraping wallpaper off my bathroom. I would have loved to have a friend in there to talk to. They wouldn't have had to lift a finger!

Sometimes we push others away because of our own fears and insecurities; for example, we use the excuse that women are "too catty." I'm the first to admit I have done this, and occasionally still do. I make all sorts of excuses to avoid the risk of rejection. It's human nature to avoid things that may harm us, but when we give into our ego's fears we are losing so much more. We are losing a little piece of ourselves. Now, I'm not suggesting you spend every waking minute with a girlfriend around, but simply to carve out more time for those we care about. It's not as hard as we make it out to be. Maybe it's time to find two or three girlfriends and make a pact. You all agree to spend a certain amount of time per week or per month hanging out. It can be with kids or without kids, it doesn't matter. The key is to make it easy, and each person holds the group accountable. It doesn't even always have to be in person, but through Facetime or another platform. You could each crack open a bottle of wine and call it "Glass of Wine Facetime." Isn't that clever? I may just use it myself!

There is something so sacred and powerful about a group of women who have each other's backs. They see each other's flaws and love every one because it has helped shape the friend they love. This circle knows you; they say, "Hell yes, you are worth it." They will listen to anything you say, except when you want to talk about what you can't do. They will lift you up and hold you accountable for what you deserve.

Maybe you used to have that circle, but because of all the things in life you've let them go by the wayside. Guess what? We all have. Stop judging yourself (or them) for it and start rekindling the group or find a new one. It's time to reunite the women in your life. You need a circle. You deserve a circle. (Or call yourself a coven, you witchy woman.) Meet regularly and start with a special ritual, how fun! It doesn't have to be so serious. You can do things that are a little different or new, even uncomfortable, because sometimes that's what really ignites our transformation. There are many such "circles of wisdom" across the country and around the world, though they gather for different reasons and around various interests. Just go on Facebook and Meetup.com, and you'll see tons of groups that honor women and bring them together, from fairy groups to workout clubs. There are no right or wrong circles. What if you got a group together and changed it up each time, like learning new things or take turns tapping into each person's passion to lead the group? Make it yours but try to be consistent with it. Meet in person as much as possible and always hold each other accountable so that everyone is empowered to reach their goals.

Circles can also help you see things from a new perspective. You might tell them how something at work is driving you so crazy, and they can empathize because it's happened to them too. Telling them helps confirm that you're not crazy. Or they might challenge you to look at the situation another way, inspiring a shift that allows you to move through it with ease. In addition, there is an energy that is created in a circle that is healing, strengthening and powerful, even if your conscious mind doesn't realize it at the time. Rest assured, something has shifted. Healing has occurred.

A friend of mine and another woman got together and decided to form a group for professional women; they would meet once a month to discuss goals and challenges. They came up with a catchy title and partnered with the local Chamber of Commerce. It spread like wildfire. Before they knew it there were groups of women meeting all over town to talk about their goals and struggles, supporting one another and enjoying the benefits of these powerful connections. Two women, one idea, one pebble thrown into the pond to create a massive impact on a community of women.

Your Circle, Your Women

As mentioned above there is no right or wrong way to create a circle; however, I do make one simple but very important suggestion: focus on joy. Ban complaining, avoid too much focus on what's not working. If all you do when you get together is laugh, you've accomplished more than you could ever know. Of course, you can talk about those struggles you face, allowing your circle to lovingly and honestly show you your blind spots, support your decisions and give perspective. The point is to empower each other, then come away with a renewed sense of who you are and what you are capable of. When you walk away from those wonderful souls, know you are blessed with a strong, divinely led group. And honor your own value, knowing they too are blessed to have you as part of their circle.

Don't feel you have to stop at one circle. You may have one circle for one reason and a separate group for another. Whether we have one group or ten, it's all about creating an environment that helps us succeed and challenges us to be who we deserve to be. If we find one circle is dragging us down, we can just release them. Maybe, like certain individuals, they were meant to be part of our journey for only a short time. It doesn't mean they aren't worthy, or that we are mean or snobby. It just means our path is leading us in a different direction. It's not personal, and if they take it as such then know that we have taken on the important role of being a mirror for them, providing them with an opportunity to deal with whatever it is that's triggering them.

Sometimes your circle takes the form of a class, like a yoga class or other learning opportunity. There was a small period of time where I felt a bit out of sorts. It wasn't really anything specific. I was worried about things that hadn't even happened; I was tired and focused on the busyness that had crept back into my life. When that happens, it can come on so slowly that we don't realize we're in a funk until it's clouding everything we do. I worked to get out of it, by meditating, reading, and writing, but it wasn't totally working. Finally, and without any real expectations, I signed up for a class, a beautiful chakra-focused class with light yoga and journeying. The teacher was earthy, funny and easy to relate to, and though I didn't know any of the other women, I immediately felt their light, loving energy. During the class, I moved my body in a slightly different way and gave myself over to an experience that allowed me to heal that wonkiness I was feeling. I felt like I was held in an energetic hug that allowed me to get back to my center. It brought back my creativity and inspiration.

I do believe that all the previous things I did – the meditation, reading, writing – helped me find my way back to myself. However, I also believe it wouldn't have been quite enough. I needed the guidance and support of others to remind me to allow the love of earth, of people, of life to pull me back into my own healing center. That circle didn't last forever – just the six weeks of the class – but it was perfect.

And Life is but a Dream...

Floating on the edge of the world, dangling on a delicate line of something and nothing...one wrong move, and she would cease to exist. She glanced up to a sky with such a radiant mix of greens, blues and purples cascading into bursts of glittery fire, and her heart yearned to be fully embraced by the beauty. But the beauty blended into the nothing, a vast darkness. She kept her breath shallow as if she had the power to keep the balance of the Universe. She looked back at them. They gave her a reassuring smile but did not reach out to help. They didn't speak but she heard their message like a whisper in her soul: *You are safe.* And she stepped into the unknown blending into the woman she was meant to be.

Conclusion

When my parents died, it sparked something in me, a desire to understand. It also created or revealed a block that presented (for me) a need to control. After much work and many tears of release, I understand that I don't control anything. I choreographed those events so I wouldn't have attachments in this life and so I could let go of the need to control or fix for others what they can (and want) to do themselves.

I have journeyed with you as you've perused these pages, asking yourself for your own truths. And I am with you in spirit. I share these words and the healing they contain, their energy. And I believe in you. You are a being filled with light and love, and you are powerful. You are magnificent. Enjoy this and every moment. You've done some great work, and you've come a long way in your life. Be proud of yourself for all the things you've done, little or big. Some have been lessons, some more fun than others but all part of your path. It's a beautiful path and it's yours to create.

I've given you some pebbles, will you throw them? I've opened the door, now it's your choice to walk through. No matter what you choose, believe in your own knowing. As we do this work, each bud within us will blossom again. And as you go deeper and deeper into yourself, you'll find it's so big and so quiet at the same time. And there's so much beauty in that. Go bravely into that dark night, allowing the process to unfold the beauty within and love yourself fiercely. And remember that there are those of us who have walked, and continue to walk, the path before you, and we promise it's worth it. ♥

In the *Wizard of Oz*, Dorothy always had the power, she just needed to learn it for herself. You too have the power. Now it's time for you to remember, to unlearn all that has kept you from who you really are. And when you do, you'll see your ruby slippers, you'll click your heels three times, and you'll know that home was always there, inside you. Waiting for you to remember your truth.

"If you know, you'll never have to ask, if you have to ask, you'll never know."

Harry Potter.

There's a dance between masculine and feminine, between soft and warrior, between doing and allowing and when I find my rhythm, when I rise into that truth, I will be free to dance the dance of the elders, on the wings of mastery, shimmering a reflection of the divine, that is, the light of pure love - our original state. This is a remembering, not a learning so go ahead, commit to the path of remembering.

Our soul,

One

single drop

In one ocean

Of energy.

Our separation,

An

Illusion.

Conclusion

Like a glacier
appearing
Separate
From its sea.
With the warmth of love
It melts
And becomes
One.
So are we,
Separated
By illusion.
And love
Melts away our fear
To bring us back
Into our
Divine Truth.

Bibliography

Cameron, J. (1992) *The Artist's Way: A Spiritual Path to Higher Creativity.* Penguin House, New York, NY.

Hicks, Jerry and Esther. (2006) *Abraham Hicks, The Law of Attraction, The Basic Teachings of Abraham.* Hay House.

Information on Salem Witch Trials. Retrieved from: http://salem.lib.virginia.edu/further.html
https://www.history.com/topics/colonial-america/salem-witch-trials

Emoto, M. (2005). *The Hidden Messages in Water.* Beyond Words Publishing, Hillsboro, Oregon.

Johnston, S.D. *Mind, Body, Spirit Practitioner Course.*

Newton, Michael, PhD. (1994) *Journey of Souls: Case Studies of Life Between Lives.* Llewelyn Publications.

Williamson, M, (1992). *A Return to Love.* Harper Collins.

Resources

Here are a few books I love that have helped me get started along my path (there are a lot more).

"The Four Agreements" by Don Miguel Ruiz

"Invoking the Archangels" by Sunny Dawn Johnston

"The Queen's Code" by Alison Armstrong

"The Five Love Languages" by Gary Chapman

"Excuse Me Your Life is Waiting" by Lynn Grabhorn

Kryon.com.

In addition to these resources, please follow YOUR heart and allow it to guide you to the books, teachings and inner teachings (that's all you, baby) that will guide you with the most ease and highest alignment with your truth along your path. There is no wrong choice, all lessons and teachings and I invite you to ask to be guided along the path of your highest potential. There is always an open door.

lisagullandnelson.com

Acknowledgements

I couldn't have done this without the support of my wonderful, accepting husband, Andy, who has willingly joined me on this crazy journey. And of course, my two children whose wholehearted acceptance has guided me to remembering our true nature as souls in this human experience. I'm grateful to all the guides and teachers both in person and in spirit who have led me to the answers and, perhaps more importantly, the questions on this part of my healing journey. And finally, to all the friends along the way who asked, "When are you going to be done with that book?" You have no idea what that has meant to me. You know who you all are. I am blessed.

www.ingramcontent.com/pod-product-compliance
Lightning Source LLC
Chambersburg PA
CBHW070950080526
44587CB00015B/2250